Praise for
It's Okay to Cry

"Open the mind of a child and you might expect to find flowers, sunshine, and Sponge Bob. Norm Wright helps us to understand that a child's world is also filled with real hurts and disappointments due to a variety of losses suffered and stored. And, after all, as Charles Dodgson (a.k.a. Lewis Carroll) so eloquently reminds us of adults, 'We are but older children, dear, who fret to find our bedtime near.' The losses of a child's world become the losses of our own psyches. *It's Okay to Cry* was more than a learning experience. It was necessary therapy."

—MIKE KLUMPP, author of *The Single Dad's Survival Guide* and father of eight

"This is a wonderfully helpful, practical book! It needs to be read by every parent, grandparent, and worker with children so we can help a generation that sees too much, is exposed to too much, and consequently knows or experiences too much—too much of everything and often not enough of their parents. This is a book that will help you be there for your child in an understanding and constructive way."

—KAY ARTHUR, CEO and cofounder of Precept Ministries International

"Every parent who has ever said a few words over a goldfish in a toilet bowl or felt the numbness of an unexpected diagnosis in a pediatrician's office will appreciate the heartfelt wisdom in *It's Okay to Cry*. Norm Wright tenderly and skillfully equips parents to help children cultivate a healthy response to life's many pains and sorrows."

—LORI BORGMAN, columnist and author of *Pass the Faith, Please*

"This is an incredible 'gift' book for all whose lives intersect grieving children. Read it with a highlighter because, sooner or later, you will need the wise counsel that Norm Wright offers. I especially found helpful his suggestions for 'An Anxiety Fable' to help children begin to find words for their losses. I will be a better grief counselor for having read this important, practical resource."

—HAROLD IVAN SMITH, CT, thanatologist and author of *When a Child
You Love Is Grieving*

It's okay to cry

It's okay to cry

A parent's guide to helping children through the losses of life

An Interactive Recovery Workbook

H. Norman Wright

WaterBrook
PRESS

IT'S OKAY TO CRY: AN INTERACTIVE RECOVERY WORKBOOK
PUBLISHED BY WATERBROOK PRESS
2375 Telstar Drive, Suite 160
Colorado Springs, Colorado 80920
A division of Random House, Inc.

Quotations from *It's Okay to Cry* © 2004 by H. Norman Wright

Scripture taken from the *Holy Bible, New International Version*®. NIV®. Copyright © 1973, 1978, 1984 by the International Bible Society. Used by permission of Zondervan Publishing House. All rights reserved.

Details in some anecdotes and stories have been changed to protect the identities of the persons involved.

ISBN 1-57856-760-2

Printed in the United States of America
2004—First Edition

10 9 8 7 6 5 4 3 2 1

Contents

Questions You May Have About This Workbook

What will the *It's Okay to Cry* workbook do for me?

Losses are momentous events in the life of every child. Grief is always about losing something 100 percent; present or future, whatever is missing has been completely taken away.

This workbook, in a practical and carefully reflective way, guides you into the knowledge and skills you need to help a child—your child—through that kind of loss. You'll explore your own experiences with loss while focusing on the many characteristics of childhood grief. You'll learn how to assist your children in the hard work of mourning until joy blossoms in their hearts once again. Best of all, you'll discover specific, practical techniques for meeting a child's needs in the midst of his or her sadness.

Is this workbook enough, or do I also need the book *It's Okay to Cry*?

Although your best approach is to read the book *It's Okay to Cry* as you go through this companion workbook, much of the text has been included here to give you a sufficiently broad and accurate indication of the book's content.

The lessons look long. Do I need to work through all of each one?

This thirteen-lesson workbook (including the introduction) is designed to promote your thorough exploration of each chapter's material, but you may find it best to focus your time on some sections and questions more than others.

Also, you may decide to follow a slower pace than one lesson per week. This could be true whether you're going through the workbook on your own or with a group. In a group that meets weekly, for example, you may decide to spend two weeks of discussion time on each lesson. (In your first meeting, decide together on what you believe to be the best pacing and schedule.) If you're going through the workbook on your own, you may simply want to try completing two or three questions each day.

Above all, keep in mind that the purpose of the workbook is to help guide you in specific life-application of the concepts and principles taught in *It's Okay to Cry*. The wide assortment of questions included in each weekly lesson is meant to help you approach this practical application from different angles and with expansive reflection and self-examination.

Allowing adequate time to prayerfully reflect on each question will be much more valuable for you than rushing through this workbook.

When Loss Comes Calling

"It makes me anxious. I'd rather avoid it.
And I don't want to make others anxious or sad either."

"When I talk about it, I start to cry. I don't like that.
Crying can make others cry, and then I feel responsible as well."

"You know, as I think about it, why should any of us know
what to say about death? No one I know talks about it."

"I don't want my children to get all morbid.
I want them to think about life, not death."

As you begin this workbook study on helping your child through loss, can you relate to some of the comments above? They were uttered by caring and concerned parents just like you. They were talking about the difficulty of facing loss and grief with their children.

1. Take a moment to settle down and center yourself as you begin. Carefully read the previous statements, and consider:

    a. Which of the statements most closely mirrors some of my own reactions when I'm face to face with loss, death, or some other grief-laden situation?

b. What events and experiences in my past might have contributed to my way of responding?

c. What is my basic attitude toward loss and the powerful feelings it can ignite?

My goal in *It's Okay to Cry* is to help you direct your children through the losses of their young lives. Yet one of our great difficulties resides in the fact that children today are sheltered from the normal transitions of life. Death is a stranger, an intruder, not a normal part of living as it was a century or two ago. It used to be that several generations lived in the same house or at least close by. The youngest children learned about birth, illness, old age, and death because these things all happened in their home. Yet today our children seem to have become a grief-free generation. All of us would prefer to avoid mourning.

In this kind of culture, then, what happens when you or your spouse has an accident, loses a job, suffers a chronic illness, or goes back to school? It's a loss for everyone, including your child. But too often we focus on the adult who is doing the losing or changing. In all the hustle to repair the damage, the youngster stands sad eyed, waiting to be noticed.

2. These are serious problems, but not insurmountable. We parents can begin by taking an inventory of our own griefs and exploring the level of our health in mourning. So consider: What does grief mean to you?

To me, grief means…

The first grief I ever experienced was…

The most difficult part of grieving is…

When I experience grief, I feel…

What I've never fully grieved over is…

What helps me the most when I am grieving is…

The way my child grieves is…

My hunches as to what things will most help my grieving child are…

Are you getting some insight into how grief affects you? Convinced that loss profoundly affects our children in similar ways (though with vast differences, too, as we shall see), we parents determine to help them. But *how?* It has to do with assisting them in the hard work of grieving. If I could sum up the theme of this book in one statement, I'd say: *Grieving our losses is essential to our ongoing emotional health, whether we're adults or children.*

Regardless of the type of loss your family has experienced, the tasks of mourning remain.

The Four Tasks of Mourning

Task 1: To accept the reality of the loss.
Task 2: To experience the pain of grief.
Task 3: To adjust to an environment in which the deceased [or other type of loss] is missing.
Task 4: To withdraw emotional energy [from the relationship with what has been lost] and reinvest it in another relationship.[1]

Actually, I like to simplify the traditional grief tasks even further so you can easily keep them in mind. They are the three steps that will help your children to grieve. Children need to (1) accept the loss, (2) experience the pain, and (3) express their sorrow.

3. Think carefully about this concept of your children needing to grieve through the three steps. In our culture, when tragedy happens in a child's life, we often hear parents and others saying: "Don't make my child go through this pain again," or "I want to save them from ever having to reexperience that!"

    a. How can reexperiencing the pain and going back through it (to mourn and cry) be the way to healing? What is your own experience with this?

    b. Think of going to the dentist with a painful toothache. But when the dentist drills, she creates even more pain! When it comes to the pain of loss, what conclusions or applications can you draw from this simple analogy?

MORE THAN LITTLE ADULTS—AND CONFUSED!

Children are different from adults in their thinking and feeling processes. Developmentally, their brains don't work like ours. Their reasoning is immature, and their understanding of the nature of cause and effect often immerses them in undue pain.

We can be of much help to our children, our precious little ones who struggle to understand what even adults will never fully comprehend. For example, children may be confused about God ("If He's so good, why did He take Mom away from us?"). They may also deal with a swirling mixture of feelings about the person who left ("If Mom really loved me, why didn't she stay here?).

And they're trying to sort through the amazing panoply of mixed messages and so-called words of wisdom they receive from grownups. One adult may be implying, *Oh, you poor little child. You must feel so sad and alone.* At the same time, someone else may be giving the message, *Now you're the man in the family. You'll have to be strong.*

So which is it?

4. Pretend that you are a six-year-old who's been raised in a Christian home, and your mother dies. Your mind is racing. List some of the questions you will wonder about. (Be sure to think and write in a six-year-old's language—or the language of your own child.)

    Who...?

    What...?

    Why...?

    When...?

    How...?

The child's memories of the deceased can also cause confusion. The survivors are talking about this person in a way that conflicts with the child's memories. *Was Mom really as perfect as they say? I didn't know that. Sometimes I didn't even like Mom, and I thought she was bad when she yelled and went on and on... I hope no one finds out what I thought!*

WILL YOU OFFER HEALTHY HELP?

Like adults, children need to relinquish and say good-bye to what they have lost. They need to accept the loss, experience the pain, and express their sorrow. They will do this differently than you will, of course. *And they will require your adult assistance*—especially in identifying and expressing the wide range of feelings they're experiencing.

I want to lay the groundwork for the specifics regarding these things (which we'll be exploring in the rest of this workbook). That groundwork involves raising three "negatives" before we even begin to uncover all the positive results that can flow from grieving and consoling one another in our families. You see, there are some decidedly unhealthy ways families deal with grief. Here are three of them to keep in mind:

- ***It's unhealthy to block emotional expression.*** This is the temptation to keep peace and calm in the family at any price. In the midst of searing loss, we attempt to keep everyone unruffled. We make sure our children are "holding up okay" or "taking it well." In this environment, outbursts of anger, hurt, or guilt will be shamed and pushed aside.

5. Could you imagine actually *encouraging* your child to have an "emotional outburst"? What would that be like for you and your family?

- ***It won't help to overprotect.*** Loving parents try to prevent their child from having to feel emotional pain. Sadly, that's impossible. The best they can do is make it seem—from outward appearances—that little Sally isn't hurting. But the pain is there; it has simply been buried so that it can fester and become more problematic in the future.

6. In what ways are you tempted to overprotect your child? (Jot down your recollections of a specific incident.)

- ***It's not good to attempt a "replacement plan."*** Many children who lose a loved one in death (a pet or person) describe it as a "big empty spot" in their life. How will you respond when this is happening in your son or daughter? If you're like most of us, you'll want to fill the void. You'll want to replace that cat or dog or goldfish, or you'll fill your child's life with toys or gadgets or experiences.

7. When you were a child, did an adult attempt a replacement plan with you? If so, how did this make you feel?

———◆———

8. As we close this introductory chapter, let's do some graphs. I'd like you to complete a Loss History Graph for yourself (see sample on page 10). On the right end of Your Loss History Graph, jot down your age today.

   The next step is to sit back and come up with your earliest recollection. Sometimes this is called the "dawn of memory." For most people, their first recollection takes them back to ages two to five. The memory could be good, bad, happy, sad, or neutral. It's just an event or experience. Then go on to plug into your graph (approximate dates are fine) the large losses during your life—for example, death of a much-loved pet, a traumatic move, death of a parent or sibling, a divorce, etc. After you complete your graph, ask yourself:
   - What am I feeling about each loss?
   - What does this tell me about the loss?

- Have I grieved over these losses or not?
- What work do I need to complete?

Susan's Graph

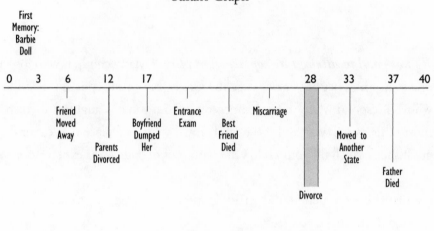

Your Loss History Graph

First Memory:

0

9. Now draw a graph for each of your children. (Use the bottom of page 11 or a separate sheet of paper, if necessary.) Follow the same instructions, and complete the losses based on the losses you were aware of. Then spend time with your children, and ask them to complete their own graphs if they're old enough. Consider:

a. Do you see any differences? Explain:

b. Do you see what you weren't aware of? Explain:

c. Do the loss graphs for your children cause you to remember and identify losses from your own childhood—perhaps some things you were never aware of prior to this exercise? Explain:

———◆———

In this introduction we've just scratched the surface of what it means to experience loss and to learn how to move through it with our children. If we've been doing some things that are mostly unhelpful or counterproductive, we can move forward to pursue the healthy alternatives. That is what we'll do together in the rest of this workbook. We'll go into much greater detail; we'll explore and expand into many related themes. But for now, simply put, here is your homework: *Give uninterrupted time to your grieving child, and listen—truly listen—to his or her concerns.*

Chapter 1

Looking Loss in the Eye

We don't talk about loss very often. As if by silent conspiracy, we seem to have an unspoken agreement not to raise the issue. We want our children to be winners. Yet with every loss comes the potential for change, growth, new insights, understanding, and refinement—all positive descriptions filled with words of hope.

So how can we help our children get through loss so these potentials might be realized? We can start by looking at the big picture. I'd like to offer three broad principles to set the stage for the specific information we'll cover in the coming pages: (1) we can let our children know that loss is normal and unavoidable, (2) we can encourage them to face loss rather than set up unhealthy "protections," and (3) we can prepare ourselves for the task by grieving our own losses in a healthy way. Let's look closer at that first point and save the other two for our next chapter.

1. How do we know that loss is normal? One reason is because the great personalities of the Bible all experienced it. So begin your study of this chapter by sitting down with your child and reading the Bible story of Joseph. As you do this, identify the different losses he experienced because of his brothers' actions.

   Now his [Joseph's] brothers had gone to graze their father's flocks near Shechem, and Israel said to Joseph, "As you know, your brothers are grazing the flocks near Shechem. Come, I am going to send you to them."

   "Very well," he replied.

So he said to him, "Go and see if all is well with your brothers and with the flocks, and bring word back to me." Then he sent him off from the Valley of Hebron.

When Joseph arrived at Shechem, a man found him wandering around in the fields and asked him, "What are you looking for?"

He replied, "I'm looking for my brothers. Can you tell me where they are grazing their flocks?"

"They have moved on from here," the man answered. "I heard them say, 'Let's go to Dothan.'"

So Joseph went after his brothers and found them near Dothan. But they saw him in the distance, and before he reached them, they plotted to kill him.

"Here comes that dreamer!" they said to each other. "Come now, let's kill him and throw him into one of these cisterns and say that a ferocious animal devoured him. Then we'll see what comes of his dreams."

When Reuben heard this, he tried to rescue him from their hands. "Let's not take his life," he said. "Don't shed any blood. Throw him into this cistern here in the desert, but don't lay a hand on him." Reuben said this to rescue him from them and take him back to his father.

So when Joseph came to his brothers, they stripped him of his robe—the richly ornamented robe he was wearing—and they took him and threw him into the cistern. Now the cistern was empty; there was no water in it.

As they sat down to eat their meal, they looked up and saw a caravan of Ishmaelites coming from Gilead. Their camels were loaded with spices, balm and myrrh, and they were on their way to take them down to Egypt.

Judah said to his brothers, "What will we gain if we kill our brother and cover up his blood? Come, let's sell him to the Ishmaelites and not lay our hands on him; after all, he is our brother, our own flesh and blood." His brothers agreed.

So when the Midianite merchants came by, his brothers pulled Joseph up out of the cistern and sold him for twenty shekels of silver to the Ishmaelites, who took him to Egypt.

When Reuben returned to the cistern and saw that Joseph was not there, he tore his clothes. He went back to his brothers and said, "The boy isn't there! Where can I turn now?"

Then they got Joseph's robe, slaughtered a goat and dipped the robe in the blood. They took the ornamented robe back to their father and said, "We found this. Examine it to see whether it is your son's robe."

He recognized it and said, "It is my son's robe! Some ferocious animal has devoured him. Joseph has surely been torn to pieces."

Then Jacob tore his clothes, put on sackcloth and mourned for his son many days. All his sons and daughters came to comfort him, but he refused to be comforted. "No," he said, "in mourning will I go down to the grave to my son. So his father wept for him.

Meanwhile, the Midianites sold Joseph in Egypt to Potiphar, one of Pharaoh's officials, the captain of the guard. (Genesis 37:12-36)

a. How might Joseph have felt at this time in his life?

b. Talk about a time when you had similar feelings. How did you handle those feelings?

c. How can other people be the most help to you when you suffer a painful loss?

Loss: Unavoidable, Frequent—and Normal

Loss occurs not just through death but by any significant change—leaving or being left, by staying in one place or moving on. How many death-losses will a person experience in his life? Ten? Perhaps twenty? But other losses can be counted in the hundreds throughout our lives. That's because loss is a normal and unavoidable fixture in our lives—as well as our children's.

2. The following is a list of changes that can create loss and grief in your child.[1] The list is not all-inclusive. You can add your own life events that you feel may create grief or anxiety in your child. Put a check mark next to the change that most closely matches your child's current life change. Then go back and put an X next to the circumstances that have affected your child significantly in the past. Jot down any events you would like to add to the list.

___ Divorce or separation of parents

___ Introduction of a stepparent

___ New sibling coming into the home

___ Extended vacation with one parent

___ Moving to a new house

___ Going to summer camp

___ Sibling leaving home

___ Death of a parent

___ Death of a grandparent

___ Death of a pet

___ Death of a friend or schoolmate

___ Illness of a loved one

___ Hospitalization of the child or a loved one

___ Starting a new school

___ Being teased or bullied

___ Being rejected by peers

___ Failing in school

___ Losing a home to fire or natural disaster
___ A friend not wanting to play anymore
___ Not making a team or club, etc.
___ Other events…

___

Now, take plenty of time to quietly meditate upon the situations you've marked. Hold the image of your child in your mind as she struggles to make sense of the situation and her attendant feelings. For each situation, answer these questions:

a. In what ways is this situation affecting my child in terms of feelings, behaviors, and beliefs?

b. What seems to be at the heart of this loss for my child?

c. What appear to be the main ways I can help my child express her feelings about this situation?

d. Beyond listening to and holding my child, what special forms of comfort can I offer at this time (and in the days ahead)?

I like to think in terms of *kinds* and *types* of losses. Let's look at both, in turn.

SOME COMMON "KINDS" OF LOSS

Consider with me some of the most common kinds of losses in the sequence most likely to occur in a child's life. Generally, it's the death of a pet, then the death of a grandparent.

Loss continues with a major move, the divorce of the child's parents, the death of a parent, the death of a playmate, friend, or relative. Or there may be a crippling injury to the child or to someone important in the child's life.

This hardly covers the gamut, of course. For example, it's a loss when you're put in an advanced class and your friends stay behind. It's also a loss if your friends are advanced and *you* stay behind! (Which of these did you experience?)

Any move can be a major loss for a child. A friend saying, "I don't want to play with you anymore" is a loss. Not making the Little League team or simply not getting to play can devastate a child. Not having a favorite dress available for a special day can be devastating for an adolescent girl. Not getting the part in a play can spoil an entire week for some kids. Sometimes the loss is a case of unexplained withdrawal of involvement by the parents.

3. As you consider the *kinds* of losses, think back through your own life history of loss. Make a list of the losses you've experienced, and ask yourself: How did I grieve through this—or not?

Some children are physically abandoned, but many more children are emotionally abandoned. Often children don't know why they feel so alone, because their parents never leave them in solitude, and their physical needs are adequately met. But their emotional needs go unmet. They lack eye contact, hugging, attentive conversation, and emotional intimacy. The verbal affirmations they so desperately need come shrouded in silence. Soon these children begin to think that something is wrong with them, and they carry this perception with them into adulthood.

And remember, the everyday losses that aren't resolved can accumulate and create anxiety, depression, and a negative attitude throughout life. The emotions of these childhood losses build up when there's no release, and someday the emotional container will overflow. For all of these reasons, Martha Wakenshaw, in *Caring for Your Grieving Child*, suggests "checking in" with your child each day.

4. What would checking in with your child look like in practical terms? Each family is different, and you can get creative with this! To prime the pump, choose one or two of the following ideas, and write out your own check-in plan that you could use regularly.

    a. Idea for preschoolers: Plan to lie on the bed with your child each night to talk about his day.
        My plan:

    b. Idea for early elementary age: Make a habit of inviting them to sit on the couch right after school and go over the day together (include events from the family's previous evening).
        My plan:

    c. Idea for elementary age: Turn check-in into a game. Say, "I'll tell you one thing I did before lunch. Then you can tell me something you did before lunch," etc.
        My plan:

    d. Idea for junior-high age: Together, each evening go over what homework tasks have been assigned. Make a point to ask something like, "How are you feeling today? How are things going for you?" (Be gentle; don't pry or nag; be ready to share your own feelings.)
        My plan:

    e. Idea for high-school age: Frequently schedule an activity together. For example, shoot some baskets in the backyard before supper. Talk…but mostly listen!
        My plan:

The Typical "Types" of Loss

I've alluded to several kinds of losses, but these actually fall into overarching categories, or types. I'll quickly group and identify at least seven so you can watch for them in your child's experience.

5. As you read through the following seven categories, think:
    a. How have I experienced this particular type of loss?

    b. What is—or will be—my child's experience of it?

    c. How can I prepare myself to be of most help to my child during this loss?

A material loss. This is a big one for any child. It could involve the loss of a physical object or even familiar surroundings. The greater the attachment, the greater the sense of loss. It's normally the first type of loss for children, or at least one they're aware of. It could be a broken toy or the fact that the dog ate their ice cream cone.

A relationship loss. Here is the end of the opportunity to relate to another person. Kids experience many of these events. When a friend isn't there, you can't talk with her, share experiences, touch, or even argue. This loss can result from a move, a divorce, or a death. It can also arise when facing cliques in school, wearing the wrong clothes, making—or not making—the team, or…just growing up.

An intrapsychic loss. With loss, a child can lose an important emotional image of herself. Not only that, her sense of what she could have become in the future is changed. The loss might force her to change cherished plans or give up a longtime dream. Often these plans and dreams have never been shared with others, so the loss that occurs is also a secret. Perhaps your daughter wants to be a dancer. And after six years of lessons she shatters her leg. Now the loss involves much more than a leg; her vision of who she is—and will be—fades into the mist.

A functional loss. We're all aware of these losses related to a muscular or neurological function of our bodies. They aren't relegated only to the old folks' home; they happen to children, too. If possible, a kid will adapt or adjust, but some functional losses can be absolutely overwhelming.

A role loss. In a family, it's the loss of an accustomed place in the relationship network. It is more or less significant depending upon how much of the person's identity was tied into this role. For example, an only child—starring at the center of family life—suddenly discovers a newborn baby sister sleeping in the room with him. He's no longer the star player. Since the old role is gone forever, it's a loss.

An ambiguous loss. This is a very difficult loss, and it comes in two prickly varieties. In the first type, family members perceive another member as physically absent but psychologically present, because it's unclear whether this person is dead or alive. It's the heartache of the missing soldier or kidnapped child. Will they indeed return someday? In the second type of ambiguous loss, a person is physically present but psychologically absent. Here is a person with Alzheimer's disease, for example, or maybe a family member has succumbed to addictions, making him numb to the family circumstances. This can happen in the family when children are young. How can they understand what's going on?

A threatened loss. One of the hardest losses of life is the threatened loss. The possibility is real; there is little to do about it. As the possibility looms, children's sense of control withers away. And for children, that loss of control hangs over their heads like a sword. It's the end of the world for them.

———◆———

As we survey the kinds and types of losses that come into our lives, one thing becomes crystal clear: Nobody likes to lose. When a loss occurs, it must mean that something is wrong…because life is supposed to be filled with winners, right? Therefore, we're tempted to do anything but let our children face the pain. Yes, we try to protect them at all costs. That is the theme we'll take up next.

6. In quietness, review what you've written and learned in this workbook chapter. As further thoughts or ideas come to mind, jot them here:

7. What for you was the most meaningful concept or truth in this chapter? How will you attempt to apply it to your life and/or the life of your children and family?

8. Take some time to hold your children in your thoughts and prayers. Consider what they need from you at the moment. What are some ways you can begin meeting their needs in the days ahead?

Chapter 2

Face the Hurt or Try to Protect?

Life is always a blending of loss and gain. Some losses are necessary for normal growth. For instance, your child discovers a tooth that starts to wiggle loose. Soon it either falls out or is pulled. But he'll learn this loss is necessary to make room for the permanent tooth. The child loses a baby tooth but gains a permanent tooth (and sometimes a little money under the pillow), and that's exciting. It pays off.

But then big losses occur, some of which may be traumatic. These cause deep pain. And that pain tempts us to protect in ways that do more harm than good.

The Great Temptation: "Protecting" Them

It's natural to want to protect our children from the hurt and sorrow of a loss. We parents do this in two main ways. First, we may begin comparing losses in order to minimize feelings. But a comparison never helps; it does just the opposite. It makes a person in grief (adult or child) feel even worse. The authors of *When Children Grieve* describe it so well: "A loss is experienced at one hundred percent. There is no such thing as half grief."[1]

1. Do you agree that comparing or minimizing is an unhealthy practice with grieving persons? Jot down some of the comparing/minimizing statements you've heard spoken to others. Then think about the *actual emotional impact* these statements would have on a listener. What are your insights about this? (The first one is done for you as an example.)

Phrase: "Don't feel bad, Kim. At least you have other grandparents."
The real impact: Kim feels ashamed for feeling bad—and guilty for (apparently) not valuing her other grandparents.

Phrase:
The real impact:

Phrase:
The real impact:

Second, parents also tend to *edit the story* of what has occurred while focusing on anticipated benefits. The hope is that life can remain as normal and pleasant as possible as we help our children not feel so bad or sad. But why is it all right to feel happy when something pleasant happens, but it's not all right to feel sad when something painful occurs? Editing the facts in order to minimize the impact of a loss can leave children feeling confused, misunderstood, and hesitant to talk about their feelings.

2. In the first set of statements that follow you'll read some creative parental edits of painful events. Study them, and then imagine rewriting them in order to affirm the legitimate feelings of hurt and sadness, as is done in the second set of statements.

   Note in the second set that the first sentence affirms the child's legitimate feelings. A follow-up statement invites the child to open up and share more feelings. Try your hand at that type of follow-up by jotting your statement in the blank provided. (An example is given.)

"Don't feel bad, Jill; this weekend we'll look for a brand-new cat."
"Don't feel bad, Fred; it was *only* a hamster!"

"Don't feel bad, Tamika; Uncle Jerry is in heaven."
"Don't feel bad, Karl; he's better off now."
"Don't feel bad, Juanita; it wasn't your fault."
"Don't feel bad, Chris; you'll do better at the next recital."
"Don't feel bad, Larnell; you did the best you could."

The rewrites…
Example: "You must be feeling pretty sad right now, Jill. <u>You really loved that cat, didn't you?</u>"

"I guess it hurts, Fred, losing your hamster like that."
Follow-up statement: _____
_____

"Feeling sad and missing Uncle Jerry, huh?"
Follow-up statement: _____
_____

"Seems like you're feeling it. Death is such a sad part of life."
Follow-up statement: _____
_____

"Feeling guilty about what happened, Juanita?"
Follow-up statement: _____
_____

"I sense that you had high expectations for your performance, Chris."
Follow-up statement: _____
_____

"You did the best you could, and it still hurts. Is that it?"

Follow-up statement: _____

_____

The point is that we can offer an invitation to our children to have and experience all of their appropriate emotions. Shutting down their hurt, anger, and sadness simply buries the emotions for resurfacing later. It also deadens their capacity for true joy.

SO…HAVE YOU FACED YOUR *OWN* HURT?

Though loss is not the enemy, it is a problem. As you continue in this book, you'll find all kinds of practical help to meet this problem. But for now, it's time to look into your own heart and begin taking inventory of your losses and how you've been dealing with them.

Take a moment to think about your life as a child. Have you identified the losses there? It's time to recognize that how we respond to losses today and tomorrow may be the result of how we responded to the early losses in our lives. All of this will affect the extent to which we are able to help our children through the losses of their lives.

3. In this workbook's introduction, you made a Loss History Graph and asked yourself some basic questions about painful past events. Now let's go a little further into that hard work of knowing, honoring, and grieving your losses. Move forward by asking yourself more specific questions, like these:

a. Reflect on one of the earliest significant losses in your life.

• When and where did this event happen?

• How old were you?

- Which people were involved?

- What are some details of what actually happened?

b. Reflect on your emotional reactions to the loss.

- What were your feelings at the time?

- How did you handle those feelings?

- To what extent did you resolve your sadness, anger, guilt?

- To what extent is the pain still with you today?

c. Recall any suggestions or advice you received on how to handle the loss.

- What did your father say?

- What did your mother say?

- What did your siblings and other relatives say?

- What did your friends say?

- What key statements have stayed with you through the years?

d. What did you learn about loss at an early age that helps you today?

e.   What did you learn then that may be hindering the way you cope with loss today?

f.   What did you learn that helps or hinders your ability to help your child through his or her losses today?

A crucial reason for completing exercises like the previous one is to be able to answer, "How do I respond to my own emotions?"

For many parents, emotions are not only confusing but are also considered a problem. Many of us were raised emotionally handicapped. We weren't given any real help with our emotional development. And what we don't feel comfortable with, we tend to fear, avoid, or resist. Then we will want to squelch the emotions in our children.

In his helpful book *The Heart of Parenting,* John Gottman talks about the two hurtful responses of either *dismissing* your child's feelings or *disapproving* of them. If you've ever responded in these ways, don't be alarmed or hard on yourself. It's possible to change. It's important to make the effort to change, though, because parents who dismiss or disapprove tend to treat their children in less than healthy ways.

ARE YOU A DISMISSING PARENT?

Parents who dismiss their child's emotions—by ignoring the feelings, disengaging from the child, or ridiculing the way the child feels—are actually saying something about themselves. You see, these reactions are especially likely when the child's emotions are so-called negative ones, because *parents often see these reflecting on themselves in some way.* They think perhaps it could mean their child is maladjusted or weak. Some go to the extreme of believing any expression of negative emotions indicates bad character traits.

When their child does express emotions, these parents feel uncomfortable, afraid, anxious, bothered, hurt, or even overwhelmed. They're afraid of getting out of control emotionally. Their natural response is, "Let's get past this emotion as quickly as possible."

But suppose they simply try to understand what the emotion *means?* If they don't, they miss a wonderful learning opportunity—and the chance to do some problem solving with their child. They also miss out on the closeness, the intimacy, that is formed when two human beings share their deepest feelings.

4. Consider what emotions in your child tend to make you uncomfortable and how these emotions tend to reflect on you.

    a. When I hear my child saying something with anger in his voice, I feel…

    b. When I observe my child being sad, I feel…

    c. When my child shows signs of fear or nervousness, I feel…

    d. Other emotions in my child that cause a significant reaction in me are…

    e. One way I'm tempted to dismiss my child's emotions is to…

OR DO YOU JUST DISAPPROVE?

If parents disapprove of the emotional expression, they are exhibiting a strong, controlling reaction. It is a critical and judgmental parental response.

Instead, when our kids share their emotions, we parents can take a positive cue: *This is a teachable moment.* This is the time to be empathetic, listening with our hearts as well as our heads. Help your child put a name to the emotion, give guidance when needed, set limits, and teach acceptable expressions. This is one of your best opportunities to teach your child how to resolve problems.[2]

5. Think carefully about whether or not you tend to disapprove of your child's emotions. Then consider:

a. What does it mean to you personally when people listen to you with their hearts as well as their heads?

b. What could you do to become more of a heart-listener with your child?

———◆———

When losses come crashing into our lives, we feel violated. Yet loss is not the enemy; not facing its existence is. Sadly, many of us have become more proficient in developing denial than in facing and accepting the losses of life. Yet we can't avoid loss or shrug it off. Even if your child tries to ignore the loss, the emotional experience is implanted in his heart and mind. No eraser will remove it; he must go through it.

There's really no mystery here: *As you learn to handle your own emotions, you can guide your children in handling theirs.* Be there to help the process along!

6. In quietness, review what you've written and learned in this workbook chapter. As further thoughts or ideas come to mind, jot them here:

7. What for you was the most meaningful concept or truth in this chapter? How will you attempt to apply it to your life and/or the life of your children and family?

8. Take some time to hold your children in your thoughts and prayers. Consider what they need from you at the moment. What are some ways you can begin meeting their needs in the days ahead?

Don't Overlook These Two!

Some losses simply get overlooked. Or their impact is severely underestimated. I'm talking about two of the most common losses of childhood: moving and losing a pet. How powerful these two events can be! They blow into our families like gale-force storms, potentially wreaking havoc in our relationships. And since they can have such a powerful impact, we do well to batten down the hatches and prepare for them while they're still on the far horizon.

MOVING: MISSING THE OLD, FAMILIAR PLACES

How often have you moved from one residence to another as an adult? What was the experience like for you (aside from all the physical labor)? You were probably exhausted, not just from the work, but from orchestrating the lives of the children at such a chaotic time. You needed to keep tabs on *people* while transferring all the *things* from one house to another. You had plenty to keep you busy and very little time to consider what this move meant to you emotionally.

1. Describe your first move. Jot down as many details as you can remember. How did this move impact you?

    What types of adjustments did you have to make?

What were your losses?

A move affects everyone emotionally, especially children. It's easy for parents to make mistakes at this time since they're feeling the pressure and perhaps staggering under the load of all that must be done. Often the last thing they want to hear from their children is…

"But I really like it here."

"Why do we have to move?"

"Leave me here, Mom, and I can live at John's house."

"I don't want to leave all my friends."

"My team needs me!"

"Everybody's going to stare at the 'new kid.' I hate that!"

2. Have your children experienced a move yet? If so, what were some of their reactions?

How were they told? What was their response—verbally, emotionally, behaviorally?

What were some signs they were adjusting to this experience?

With the arrival of the moving van, a child is leaving his world as he knows it. And in the fiery heat of change, certain parental mistakes are sure to bubble to the surface. Here are a few to avoid.

Mistake: Focusing only on the new. But what about the old—the old place, the old school, the old friends? Are children supposed to immediately erase their memory? Are they supposed to be just as excited as their parents about the new job challenge, the lovely french doors, or the incredibly low mortgage rate?

No. Those are adult concerns.

3. In the following space, list some of the exciting aspects—for adults—of moving to a new place. Put an asterisk next to any items that would also be exciting for children. What are your insights about the relative importance of "the new" to your child?

Mistake: Avoiding the physical and emotional prep work. This kind of preparation involves saying good-bye to the old—at church, preschool or school, and at the old house. For years I've suggested that, as a family, you go from room to room in the house, talk about your favorite memories in each room, and say good-bye to each room. You could even encourage your children to write a letter to your house or backyard, thanking it for all the good times and saying good-bye to each place. Children could leave a letter in each room or read the letter to each room.

4. If your family is planning a move, how would your children prefer to say good-bye to the old places, friends, circumstances? Plan to talk this through together, and note your plans here:

Mistake: Overlooking the impact of differing cultures. A family moved from the thriving metropolis of Denver to a tiny town in Arkansas. For six months the five had to live in a small condo while their new home was being built. What a different culture they encountered in the small southern city—the focus on agriculture, rodeo, and guns; the different way of talking; the miniature school-class sizes; the folksy, unhurried conversations; the unusual weather patterns; and—as all the girls quickly pointed out—the bugs! This move just wasn't pleasant, and there were multiple intangible losses.

5. What could be some of the intangible losses mentioned in the previous paragraph?

Mistake: Minimizing the apparently "smaller" loss. If the move results from a family breakup due to divorce or death, an abundance of losses will follow. In the midst of these, it would be easy to overlook the losses tied to the move. That is, it's no good focusing just on the "big" losses while letting the seemingly smaller ones take their course. As we learned in the previous chapter, all losses are experienced at 100 percent; there is no "half grief."

Mistake: Never really talking it through. Share your own feelings to let your children know it's all right to talk about this move. Some of the kids might be very angry toward you (or those responsible for "making" them move).

6. Once you decide to open up the lines of communication about your move, how will you begin? Some parents start like this:

"I'm looking forward to this move, because _____. But I'm also sad since I will be leaving _____."

"I'm not looking forward to this move, because _____. But we have to do it. Let's talk about why we don't like moving."

How would you fill in those blanks?

After making a statement like one of those, you and your children can move on to discuss what you could all look forward to and how you could work together to make the move better.

PETS: WHEN ROVER GOES AWAY

"It's just a pet. Don't be so upset."

"You knew it had to die someday, so you should have been ready for this."

"Hey, real people have died in this family; so what's the big deal about Fluffy?"

Sadly, such statements abound in our families. And the words sear the hearts of children who have lost a pet they truly loved. Viewing a floating goldfish (remember?) can be upsetting—even if Grandpa died just last month. The pet still counts; its death still hurts.

7. Below, list the pets you had as a child:

How did they die?

Do you remember your reactions and your feelings? List them:

What did others say to you when your pets died?

Try to see it from the child's point of view. Children often bond to their pets more than their parents bond to those animals. They form deep, emotional attachments to their dog or cat or hamster or guinea pig. They provide the pet with the best of care, and some children and pets are inseparable. An only child may even view the pet as a sibling. A sick child may see a pet as a source of comfort and protection. After all, a pet will play with a child when others won't. Children, in particular, are at risk for a significant amount of grief with a pet loss—whether it comes from dying, getting lost, or going with the other household in a divorce.

8. If your family has recently lost a pet, here are some ways you can begin talking about it with your child:

_____ Let's talk about the first time we all saw our pet, Snowball. Let's write down our memories of the first time.

_____ Let's all draw a picture of Snowball.

_____ What was our favorite experience or most fun experience with Snowball?

_____ Who in our family did Snowball look like and act like the most?

_____ When Snowball died, what did we think and feel?

Place a check mark next to the approach that seems like the best way for you to begin. Jot a brief prayer for God's help here:

When a pet dies, keep in mind that this could be the first personal friend of your child to die. And it will also be one of his first learning experiences about illness and death. That's the potentially positive note: The grief your child experiences over this loss teaches that death is part of the process of life. All of us will need to learn that sooner or later.

How can you help when Rover is no more? Let me suggest a few basic dos and don'ts.

- DO face your own grief.
- DON'T "fudge" the truth.
- DO make room for questions—all of them.
- DON'T neglect good-byes in word and deed.
- DO remember to keep checking in.
- DON'T forget to enlist others.

9. As you consider this list of dos and don'ts, think about how each best relates to your particular situation. What practical action can you take with regard to one of these guidelines?

LET'S REMEMBER OUR PET

Use the following outline as a simple discussion guide when talking with your child about a pet that has died. Use your own words, though, and keep the conversation as natural as possible. Remember, these questions are only suggestions to help you get started. Your child may take the conversation along different paths. Be ready to follow where he or she leads.

- Let's talk about _____. I wonder what her name meant to you.
- I wonder what you said to _____ that you could share with me.
- Did you celebrate _____'s birthday? How?
- What do you wish you could have said to _____ before she died?
- Did she ever talk to you? If so, what did she say?
- Was _____ a member of our family? How could you tell?

- I wonder which of these happened to you? Did _____
  …love you? How do you know?
  …make you feel needed and important? Talk about it.
  …comfort you when you were sad? If so, how?
  …ever get angry with you? What happened?
  …help you be more responsible? If so, how?
- How could you say good-bye to _____?

———◆———

When it comes to the loss of a pet—or all the losses that come with moving—the key is to remember that *each child will grieve in a different way and for a different amount of time.* If the intense sadness or anger goes on for more than five or six months, however, you may want to seek professional help. As for immediately replacing Rover? No. Don't obtain a new pet right away, even if your child pressures you for one. The grieving process needs time.

10. In quietness, review what you've written and learned in this workbook chapter. As further thoughts or ideas come to mind, jot them here:

11. What for you was the most meaningful concept or truth in this chapter? How will you attempt to apply it to your life and/or the life of your children and family?

12. Take some time to hold your children in your thoughts and prayers. Consider what they need from you at the moment. What are some ways you can begin meeting their needs in the days ahead?

Chapter 4

Sickness...and All Its Big Questions

Are you in the midst of a health crisis right now in your own family? Or maybe you've been there in the past. If not, you may well face such a situation in the future.

In any case, I believe such traumatic circumstances raise critical questions in every parent's thinking. Will you allow me to anticipate and answer some of those questions? I've organized this workbook chapter around Three Big Questions I often hear when a family's major loss is all about being sick.

BIG QUESTION #1: WHAT ARE THE SPECIAL CHALLENGES OF CHRONIC ILLNESS?

None of us wants our children to be sick with any disorder, let alone a chronic illness. But it may happen. And here's what's so important to know: As the parent, you will be the key person assisting your child through the loss process.

It will be you, not the doctor.

One mother finally realized how much of a challenge and a calling her child's illness would be to her. At age five, her boy was diagnosed with spinal muscular atrophy, a form of muscular dystrophy. She puts it like this: "I got mail from the Muscular Dystrophy Society and threw it away for a whole year. I was a basket case. Although my family couldn't have been more supportive, I kept thinking, *You don't know what I am going through.*"[1]

Of course, we expect children to be under the weather once in a while. But on the other hand, chronic illnesses—conditions with a long duration or recurring quality—are strictly for the kid down the block, right? It's not supposed to happen to us! Such circumstances can change family routines as life centers around hospital visits or the giving of meds or extensive trips to the specialist.

1. Do you agree that, with chronic illness, you (rather than the doctor) will be the "key person assisting your child through the loss process"? If so, think it through: What aspects of such a situation would (or do) make you a basket case? Make a short list here:

   • Having to schedule ongoing doctor/therapy appointments...
   • Needing to arrange a more flexible schedule at work...

   • Other:

   • Other:

   • Other:

   • Other:

   • Other:

As a parent, you will be in shock when you hear the diagnosis of a serious disease or disorder. Your head will spin with a sense of disbelief, of unreality. *This happens to other children, not us.* And your first response may be to distance yourself from the news: *It must be wrong. The doctor's mistaken. It's someone else's child.* The diagnosis itself is a major loss for you as well as your child.

Then comes the pain of hearing about the treatment, and finally you listen to the doctor's prediction about your future: the prognosis. The more complex any of these three elements are, the more of a roller-coaster ride you're in for as the parent.

2. Look back at the list you created in question 1. Why not make it a prayer list for courage and strength, whether you are facing the crisis now or need to prepare yourself for that future possibility? (Suggestion: Stop and spend some moments now in silent prayer with your list.)

Big Question #2: What's Going to Happen When a Serious Illness Hits My Child?

There's no easy way to say this: Now much of your life will revolve around your child's illness and its effects. There will be special meals, cancelled vacations, a change in living conditions, trips to the doctor or hospital or pharmacy, searches for as much information and help as you can find. Your child with the illness experiences losses, you experience losses, and so do the other children in the household. Their needs don't change, but your time, attention, and energy do. A child's illness can impact your marriage and your job as well.

Actually, you're called on to transform your role. You were the parent of a healthy child. Now you're thrust into the role of a parent of a seriously ill, chronically ill, or disabled child.[2]

You will need to face your emerging fears at this time. You will probably be afraid that your child will suffer horribly, that he or she won't recover, that you can't handle all the responsibility, and that your child may die (even if nothing has been said about this). If your child is terminal, you'll likely fear that you won't be able to handle the grief.[3]

3. Look at a few phrases drawn from the previous three paragraphs. Think about how each phrase impacts you emotionally. How does each phrase relate to your experience?

    a. "much of your life"

b. "impact your marriage and your job"

c. "face your emerging fears"

d. "can't handle all the responsibility"

e. "afraid…your child may die"

So…what's going to happen when serious illness hits your family? Life as you know it will be over. You'll take up a new life—a scary, busy, new life filled with incredible challenges. It may well be filled with awesome blessings, too, as so many parents of faith and courage have testified.

BIG QUESTION #3: WHAT'S IT ACTUALLY LIKE FOR MY SUFFERING CHILD?

When children are sick, their fear grows.

"When do I get better?"

"What's going to happen to me today?"

"Is this going to really hurt?"

"Who is this new person?"

"What are they going to do now?"

One five-year-old boy was very open about his condition and would tell everyone, "I have spinal muscular atrophy, and it makes my muscles weak, and if I can't walk right or if I fall, it's not my fault. If you have any questions, just ask me." He had a friend with the same condition who wouldn't talk about the problem nor let anyone help him.

Children do vary in their acceptance of their illness. Let's look at three of the younger ages separately.

Infants. Even the youngest children will be significantly affected by your stress and anxiety. So remember that it's very easy to transfer emotions to children; it seems to rub off onto them. How will you know? They may become unresponsive. Or, lacking verbal ability, they may express discomfort through irritability or fretfulness. Along with these possible responses, your children may become overly attached to you—clinging and not wanting the care of others.

4.   Since your emotional state has such an impact on your children, it's important to nurture your soul daily, to care for your emotional self. Why not go to the Scriptures for help? Here are six Bible passages (dealing with worry, anxiety, and fear) for you to read and meditate upon this week. Ask God to speak to your heart through these words, and feel free to write your prayerful responses in the spaces provided.

> The LORD is my light and my salvation—
>   whom shall I fear?
> The LORD is the stronghold of my life—
>   of whom shall I be afraid?
> When evil men advance against me
>   to devour my flesh,
> when my enemies and my foes attack me,
>   they will stumble and fall.

Though an army besiege me,
    my heart will not fear;
though war break out against me,
    even then will I be confident. (Psalm 27:1-3)

Therefore I tell you, do not worry about your life, what you will eat or drink; or about your body, what you will wear. Is not life more important than food, and the body more important than clothes? Look at the birds of the air; they do not sow or reap or store away in barns, and yet your heavenly Father feeds them. Are you not much more valuable than they? Who of you by worrying can add a single hour to his life? (Matthew 6:25-27)

For in this hope we were saved. But hope that is seen is no hope at all. Who hopes for what he already has? But if we hope for what we do not yet have, we wait for it patiently.

In the same way, the Spirit helps us in our weakness. We do not know what we ought to pray for, but the Spirit himself intercedes for us with groans that words cannot express. And he who searches our hearts knows the mind of the Spirit, because the Spirit intercedes for the saints in accordance with God's will. (Romans 8:24-27)

Do not be anxious about anything, but in everything, by prayer and petition, with thanksgiving, present your requests to God. And the peace of God, which transcends all understanding, will guard your hearts and your minds in Christ Jesus. (Philippians 4:6-7)

For God did not give us a spirit of timidity, but a spirit of power, of love and of self-discipline. (2 Timothy 1:7)

Then I saw a new heaven and a new earth, for the first heaven and the first earth had passed away, and there was no longer any sea. I saw the Holy City, the new Jerusalem, coming down out of heaven from God, prepared as a bride beautifully dressed for her husband. And I heard a loud voice from the throne saying, "Now the dwelling of God is with men, and he will live with them. They will be his people, and God himself will be with them and be their God. He will wipe every tear from their eyes. There will be no more death or mourning or crying or pain, for the old order of things has passed away." (Revelation 21:1-4)

Toddlers. Toddlers can be frustrated by illness; it limits their main goal in life: exploration. Constant doctor and therapy visits can produce angry responses. Children at this age level will sense your moods as well. Toddlers have limited language skills with which to express themselves, but they can understand many of your words. So you need to be careful what you say around them to friends, family, the doctor, nurse, and anyone over the phone. At this age, illness can lead to tantrums and throwing toys. The toddler has lost his freedom and ability to explore when he's sick.

5. Think it over carefully: What kinds of things would you definitely *not* want your toddler to overhear you saying when he or she is sick, injured, or chronically ill?

Preschoolers. Can illness or disability be explained to the preschool age group? Yes, since they can begin to understand *the process.* Sometimes pictures, picture books, or stories can convey a limited message. Or you may need to create your own visual aids.

When you go to urgent care, the doctor, the hospital, or a therapist, have the practitioner explain in your child's vocabulary what is occurring. You may not fully know how much your child can understand, but make the attempt to convey everything clearly and with emotional equilibrium.

Preschoolers are quite aware of their bodies, so anything that affects their bodies will be the focus of their attention. This is where magical thinking—their belief that their own thoughts can influence people and events—comes into play, along with a skewed sense of cause and effect. As one child said, "I didn't take my nap the other day; that's why I got sick. Today if I take my nap, my sick will go away." Another child stated, "I told my tummy to hurt so I could stay home. I shouldn't tell it that 'cause now it hurts. I don't want to hurt like this. I have to tell it to stop hurting, and it will." At this age, kids believe their words and actions have so much power!

6. What practical things can we do to help our children cope, no matter how old they are? The most important thing I can say is this: *You know your children better than anyone else; proceed with creative and prayerful common sense.* As examples, I've outlined four different ideas you could try. Consider each one, and in the spaces provided make any notes about how you could implement one or more of them.

    Idea: Ask your children to draw how they feel when they're sick (with a cold or flu). Have them describe what this means, and then post the drawing on their door until they're well.

Idea: Play the game "I don't like being sick because…" Have your child complete the phrase; then you complete the phrase. Repeat the process several times. Record the answers for both of you.

Child: "I don't like being sick because…
Parent: I don't like being sick because…
Child: "I don't like being sick because…
Parent: I don't like being sick because…

Pray together for God to make your child well. And when he's better, thank God for this!

Idea: Have a story time. For example, "Jimmy was a little boy who got sick. He had the _____. Do you know what the _____ is? (If your child doesn't know, tell her). Because he had this sickness, he had to stay home from preschool. After two days (months, years) he said, 'I don't like being sick because I miss out on _____.'" (Have your child finish the sentence; use any other sentence-completion statements that can help open the door for the free expression of feelings.)

Idea: When you have frequent doctor visits, invite your child to try the following:

a. Draw a picture of her doctor.
b. Draw a picture of one of the nurses.
c. Make a list of questions to ask the doctor, such as:
   What's a cold?
   What's a germ?
   What does a germ look like?
   How do I get germs?

What do you hear when you listen to my chest?

Why do shots hurt?

———◆———

When children are sick or chronically ill, the questions swirl endlessly and seem to multiply as the difficulties deepen. Be ready to answer each question with truthful responses in kid-friendly language. Then be ready to answer those questions all over again. Ask God for patience and perseverance as you move into each new day, and rely on His strength.

7. In quietness, review what you've written and learned in this workbook chapter. As further thoughts or ideas come to mind, jot them here:

8. What for you was the most meaningful concept or truth in this chapter? How will you attempt to apply it to your life and/or the life of your children and family?

9. Take some time to hold your children in your thoughts and prayers. Consider what they need from you at the moment. What are some ways you can begin meeting their needs in the days ahead?

Chapter 5

In the Family "Machine"— Each Part Affected!

Who helps parents know how to respond to the *other* children when their sibling is chronically ill or deceased? Thankfully, research is providing parents with helpful information about what to expect when there's a sick or disabled child in the family. Now we can prepare for the complex reactions that tend to reverberate through the family system.

We need to become experts at interpersonal responses and reactions. We might even view the family as a kind of flesh-and-blood machine with myriad working parts and processes. If one part goes off kilter—gets damaged or completely broken—can we predict how the rest of the machinery will respond?

Yes! Let's stand back and observe that struggling machine to see what happens. How will it function now? What actions and reactions will become evident, spurred by the weakened or missing part? In the family, when a child is sick or dies, the reactions have to do with *how everybody else is affected and how they'll respond.*

1. When another family member is sick, what are some of the losses your *well* children may experience?

2. What does the Bible say in the following verses that you can do with your child when he is sick?

> Is any one of you sick? He should call the elders of the church to pray over him and anoint him with oil in the name of the Lord. And the prayer offered in faith will make the sick person well; the Lord will raise him up. If he has sinned, he will be forgiven. (James 5:14-15)

How the Siblings Might Act and React

Children are greatly affected when one of their siblings is sick or disabled. They have a greater-than-usual level of neediness. They want more nurturing from their parents at a time when their parents have less to give. When a loss or crisis occurs, too often no one thinks about talking to the other children about what's going on and why. Consequently, they continue to struggle with their feelings, their questions, and their emotional pain. They may feel alone and quite angry. Other responses you may notice in the siblings are…

- feeling increased pressure to overachieve, compensating for the "helpless" brother or sister;
- needing to cope with parents' requests to help care for the special-needs brother or sister;
- having a greater sense of needing to fulfill the parents' hopes and dreams for success in their children;
- experiencing guilt about "passing" an older, disabled brother or sister in skills and abilities.

3. Do you notice any of the previous reactions in your well children? Place a star next to the bulleted point that you'll need to watch for in the future.

But suppose you don't see much of a change in your other children? This could happen. Many children hide their distress and have to deal with it years later in adulthood. Be alert to the child who seems quiet and unaffected. Come alongside and gently, as the time passes, keep providing opportunities for emotional expression.

Finally, remember that children raised with a disabled sibling often feel a strong sense of responsibility, either self-imposed or placed on them by their parents. Therefore, you may see very positive changes as the child decides to be "the good daughter." It is her means of survival. She makes few demands on her exhausted and stressed parents, and she tries to be helpful. But she, too, has needs her parents must meet. She also requires an opportunity to grieve.

How Parents Might Respond to the Siblings

You may be aware that you're not doing what you want or need to do with the other children. Your grief drains your energy and the emotional investment you want to make in them. So you feel you're not being the parents you want to be, which adds to your frustration and sense of failure. But remember this: It's unrealistic to think you can act the way you want with the other children. You just don't have enough to give.

You'll also fluctuate in your feelings and responses to your children. You may feel resentment that your other children are healthy or still living, don't seem to be as concerned or grieving enough, or have adjusted too soon. Part of your response is your anger over the unfairness of what has happened. You may feel that you can't invest what you want or that you've lost your ability to give. Or you may be afraid to invest because something bad could happen to these children. You could also overreact and overprotect. I raise all of these possible difficulties, because just being aware of them may help you avoid them.[1]

4. We tend to think that only major or chronic illnesses disrupt a family or put pressure on the parents. But what if your child has a cold every month for ten months in a row? Your life changes dramatically with each illness. So do your patience, stamina, and even your church attendance. Here are some questions to help you reflect on this type of loss. Complete each sentence:

An illness I had as a preschooler was…

An illness I had in elementary school was…

My worst illness was…

When I was sick, my mom…

When I was sick, my dad…

The losses I experienced when I was sick were…

When my child is sick, I feel…

What my child needs from me when he or she is sick is…

Now that you've completed these statements, what did you learn about you *and* your child?

What are your insights about how you can best help your child handle an illness or injury in the future?

How Siblings Might React to the Sick Child

Siblings face numerous pressures we don't even think about. What does a child say to others when asked about a younger brother who just died? What does a child say to others when asked about a sibling who doesn't look disabled in any way but is nonverbal? Sometimes the less severe the impairment, the more difficult it is for the siblings, since they may feel embarrassed about their brother's or sister's behavior.

We wondered how Matthew, our retarded son, affected our daughter, Sheryl. (Matthew was born with his disability several years after Sheryl. When Matthew died at twenty-two, he was about eighteen months old mentally.) She seemed to handle his presence all right, but we weren't always sure.

When Sheryl was about thirty, I asked her how Matthew had affected her and what problems she had experienced in having a disabled brother. Here's her response: "I can't think of any problems I had with Matthew being retarded when I was young.... But when I became an adult, I understood. Then it was difficult to deal with. I couldn't handle going to Matthew's home and seeing all the other disabled children. It just tore me to pieces. I have a difficult time seeing retarded children now."

I told Sheryl that I understood and have a similar response and sensitivity to seeing anyone with a disability. It took me years to discover that what I was feeling was the wish that I could reach out and heal that person—make him or her whole—followed by the frustration of knowing I couldn't do it. Sheryl floored me with her response: "I don't think Matthew's retardation was something for us to try to heal. I think his purpose was to bring healing to all of us. We're all different because of him. I know I'm a different person because of Matthew."

5. What is your reaction to Sheryl's statements?

Have you ever felt that a severe disability (or form of adversity) could be a source of healing? If so, how might this principle apply in your current circumstances?

How a Deceased Child Affects Everyone

Can there be any emotional pain worse than that of losing one's child? Yet because of this, parents commonly shut down and respond in silence and secrecy regarding the child's death. This leaves the remaining children feeling haunted by their deceased sibling. They feel they must seal up their feelings, positive or negative, toward their lost sibling. If they had an enjoyable and close relationship, that bond must stay buried. If they had ongoing, unresolved conflicts, those too must stay buried. The children end up grieving alone.

Why the silence? What are parents afraid to talk about? Usually it's blame, the shared feeling that they could have done something to prevent the death. Children, with their limited understanding and resources, wonder why they can't talk about it. They may conclude that their parents are angry at them and that the sibling's death is their own fault. This is especially true if the siblings didn't get along prior to the child's death. And so we end up with a situation in which the children *won't* talk because it would upset the parents, and the parents *don't* talk because it would upset the children. Everyone is busy protecting everyone else. But this kind of protection brings no healing.

6. At this point, let's pause for a moment to look at your history with death. Complete the following sentences. (If you're married, ask your spouse to complete these sentences as well. Then discuss your responses.)

    *   The first death I experienced was...

    *   The way I was told about death was...

    *   The first funeral I attended was...

    *   What I remember about the funeral and the questions I had were...

    *   The ways I was prepared for what I'd see at the funeral was...

- My childhood beliefs or superstitions about death included…

- What I think my child knows about death at this time is…

- If my child were to ask me about heaven, I would say…

- Some of the questions I hope my child *doesn't* ask me about death and the afterlife are… (Note: Be ready. Prepare your answers!)

One of the crucial struggles for young children is reconciling what they know about death (for instance, it only happens to old people) with the death of a sibling or playmate close to their age. That's why so often a young child will talk about the "should haves." They may say again and again, "I should have…"

Help them finish the statement. It could be "I should have stopped him…;" "I should have helped him…;" "I should have told him…"

And what about fears? Children who lose a sibling can experience a number of fears, including:

- Fear of losing you, other siblings, or grandparents. They tend to see the remaining people as candidates for death.
- Fear of their own death, especially if they were younger than a sibling who died, and they're approaching the age at which he or she died.
- Fear of going to sleep, because they equate sleep with death. Dreams and nightmares intensify the fear.
- Fear of separation because of the perceived insecurity of the home and family.

7. Which of the four previous fears seems most likely to plague your children? What forms of comfort and help could you offer?

———◆———

Amid all of these painful situations and aching questions, there is much hope for the grieving family. Remember, no one can provide a quick cure for loss and grief. You, as a family, must make your unique pathway through the pain. I only invite you to remember that with grief, as with any crushing adversity we face in life, the best way *out* is always *through*.

8. In quietness, review what you've written and learned in this workbook chapter. As further thoughts or ideas come to mind, jot them here:

9. What for you was the most meaningful concept or truth in this chapter? How will you attempt to apply it to your life and/or the life of your children and family?

10. Take some time to hold your children in your thoughts and prayers. Consider what they need from you at the moment. What are some of the ways you can begin meeting their needs in the days ahead?

Chapter 6

The Grieving Family:
Roles, Rules, and Responses

Like a ship sailing into heavy winds, sometimes the family system gets tossed around, buffeted, even severely damaged. It flounders off course or loses its trim, especially when it sails headlong into devastating loss. Yet if a family is prepared and skillful, it can adjust to the threatening conditions. It can make the moves necessary to keep everything in balance, even as it's weathering the worst of times. Is your family like that?

DISCERNING THE DIFFERING ROLES

We can observe some typical ways families successfully navigate through grief to reach their new state of equilibrium. For one thing, they realize that their members will take on differing *roles*. They also learn what to expect when it comes to family *rules* and *responses* in crisis. Most important, they're able to adopt survival *attitudes* based upon principles that have stood the test of time.

1. Who are your family members? Write their names on the next page, including grandparents (living or deceased), and note their primary roles and expectations. (Optional: On separate sheets of paper, invite your child to draw a picture of every family member.)

Name: *Primary Role:*

Name: *Primary Role:*

Name: *Primary Role:*

Name: *Primary Role:*

Name: *Primary Role:*

Name: *Primary Role:*

Name: *Primary Role:*

Name: *Primary Role:*

When everyone has an appropriate role to play, the family can maintain equilibrium. It can all work quite well. The downside is that sometimes roles aren't assigned suitably, which creates serious consequences. What if a child is given a role that's inappropriate, such as expecting a daughter to take on her deceased sister's personality or asking an eight-year-old boy to be the man of the house now that his dad is gone? Beware of such assignments. A new role can hold multiple gains…and severe losses.

2. In light of the roles you've just noted, consider:

    a. Are all of the assigned roles appropriate for each adult and child? If not, what is unhealthy and/or what should change?

b. With the loss your family has experienced (death, sickness, etc.), how do individual roles need to be adjusted?

c. What are some of the possibilities and dangers of the adjustments you are planning? (As a family, talk it through together!)

WHAT ARE THE RULES AROUND HERE?

Along with roles, every family has rules. Here are some of the things parents often "tell" their children. These rules come through whether in spoken words or in the general atmosphere and ordering of family interactions:

- You must make me happy.
- Don't get excited (or angry, sad, fearful, etc.). Such emotions threaten to unblock my own tightly controlled feelings.
- Your job is to take care of me.
- You will be loved if you perform up to the standards.
- Walk on eggshells.
- Keep things orderly and calm around here.
- Live in denial.
- Don't speak the truth if it will make any of us feel bad.
- We must not openly grieve our dead loved ones; it's too painful for us.
- We must not touch one another. It could lead to problems.
- If you need something, I'll give it to you. I know your needs better than you do.[1]

3. It's when losses hit that some of the most longstanding and cherished rules are finally forced into the open. So take a look at your family's expression of feelings.

Read the following list, and circle those feelings you are personally comfortable with. Underline those that are difficult for you to experience and/or express or to observe others expressing. Place a check by those you observe in your child. For those you don't see your child experiencing or expressing, what might be the reason? Think: *Is there a rule in place here?*

afraid	lonely
angry	sad
confused	depressed
anxious	guilty
ashamed	frustrated
discouraged	embarrassed
happy	hurt
elated	excited
isolated	dejected

(Suggestion: Ask other family members to answer the same questions, and then discuss your responses. Keep in mind that our children will probably express the very feelings we have never resolved in our own lives.)

A healthy family, and one that recovers sooner, allows all its members to know, have, and express their feelings in an appropriate manner. Then, after the chaotic upheaval of significant loss, the goal is to reach a new state of balance in your family. If the rules are restrictive and burdensome, it becomes more difficult to do so. If the rules are aired and pared down to acceptable levels for all, then you can begin working on your new way of life together.

GET READY FOR UNIQUE RESPONSES!

It's easy for us parents to try to set the record straight so that every family member will respond to the missing (or sick) one in the same way. However, *you can't expect a child to respond the way you do.* Yes, it would be so much easier if family members all grieved the same way and in a healthy fashion. But they don't, and sometimes they keep others from working through their own grief as well. Let's consider the different family roles and whether any family members can be identified.

4. Here are some statements you may have heard in your family after a death or other significant loss.[2] Each one reflects a family style. Without passing judgment, think about who may fall into a style, and consider that style's impact on the rest of the family members.

   a. A family member announces, "This isn't anything we should talk about again." (She attempts to control everyone in the family by imposing a universal gag rule. She blocks others in their expressions of grief.)

   <u>Name(s) of family member(s) this fits</u>   <u>Impact on others</u>

   b. Another says, "Of course you can talk about it—but not with me." (Members in this family may grieve, but they end up doing it alone.)

Name(s) of family member(s) this fits   Impact on others

c. Another may be responding to everyone who asks, "We are doing just fine, just fine, but thanks for asking." (Yet the child and others may hardly be doing fine!)

Name(s) of family member(s) this fits   Impact on others

d. Another may respond with anger: "This is just one more thing we have to deal with! Why do things like this always happen to this family!" (Family members may not express their grief, in order to keep the peace.)

Name(s) of family member(s) this fits   Impact on others

e. Another responds with shallow platitudes: "Oh, let's not be sad about this. Our faith is all we need, and it's going to see us through." (There is truth in this, but if sadness isn't allowed, the grief is buried, waiting to erupt someday. This is a form of denial.)

Name(s) of family member(s) this fits   Impact on others

Just imagine a child who has experienced a major loss and hears these various responses from his mother, father, older siblings, and extended family members. What is he to believe about grief? How is he to act?

You can be the one to help him.

5. If a number of individuals are on "different pages" in their grief styles, what first, small steps could you take to help move the family to a new page that's healthier? (Note: Be practical but realistic.)

SNAPSHOT OF SURVIVAL: A TOP SEVEN LIST

How can families adjust to their losses...and survive? Each family is unique in its specific coping responses; however, we can identify some key characteristics of the surviving family. This "top seven" list offers a quick summary.

1. Surviving families learn from others who've made it.
2. Surviving families express their emotions in healthy ways, recognizing that tears are a gift from God that don't need apology.
3. Surviving families look for solutions rather than create a war zone of blame.
4. Surviving families don't magnify their problems, nor do they get stuck using victim phrases, such as *I can't... I'll never... If only...*
5. Surviving families don't allow themselves to become bitter, refusing to live in the past or to focus on "the unfairness."
6. Surviving families resolve their conflicts. New conflicts aren't automatically contaminated by a reservoir of past unresolved issues. (If a family hasn't learned to resolve conflicts *before* a crisis, it's not likely to do it *during* one.)
7. Surviving families cultivate a biblical attitude toward life.

In this survival list, each item is important. But I want to stress the final one, the one that should really go at the top of the list: *cultivating a biblical attitude.* Why is attitude so important? It's because some crises you know you will experience in life, but other crises take you totally by surprise. That's when you face the crucial decision: How will I interpret this event?

6. So many events in or near my life I never anticipated. I've listed two of my never-expecteds to start you thinking about your own. After my examples, complete your own list of never-expected statements in the spaces provided. When you're done, prayerfully consider: *How did I choose to interpret this situation? In what ways were my choices helpful or harmful to me and others?*

   • I never expected to have a son born profoundly mentally retarded with brain damage and then suddenly die at the age of twenty-two. But it happened.
   • I never expected that my daughter, at the age of twenty, would take a detour in her Christian life and live with boyfriends, use cocaine, and move into alcoholism. But it happened and continued for four years.
   • I never expected…

   • I never expected…

   • I never expected…

   • I never expected…

As we've faced crises and losses over the years, my wife and I have relied upon many promises in God's Word. One passage in particular came alive as we depended on it more and more:

Consider it pure joy, my brothers, whenever you face trials of many kinds, because you know that the testing of your faith develops perseverance. Perseverance must finish its work so that you may be mature and complete, not lacking anything. (James 1:2-4)

We've found that learning to put that attitude into practice is a process. The passage does not say, "respond this way *immediately*." We apparently have to feel the pain and grief first, and then we'll be able to consider it all joy.

The key is to remember that *you have the power to decide what your attitude will be.* Don't deny the pain or hurt you might have to go through, but ask: "What can I learn from this? How can I grow through this? How can I use it for God's glory?"

7. Pain and suffering are not good; they are loathsome aspects of a warped creation that will be with us until God's kingdom fully arrives. However, suffering can be redeemed to some extent in this life. When have you most clearly seen this principle at work in your life?

Can you pause for a moment and give thanks? (Note: Read the following before responding.)

"My grace is sufficient for you, for my power is made perfect in weakness." Therefore I will boast all the more gladly about my weaknesses, so that Christ's power may rest on me. That is why, for Christ's sake, I delight in weaknesses, in insults, in hardships, in persecutions, in difficulties. For when I am weak, then I am strong. (2 Corinthians 12:9-10)

8. In quietness, review what you've written and learned in this workbook chapter. As further thoughts or ideas come to mind, jot them down here:

9. What for you was the most meaningful concept or truth in this chapter? How will you attempt to apply it to your life and/or the life of your children and family?

10. Take some time to hold your children in your thoughts and prayers. Consider what they need from you at the moment. What are some of the ways you can begin meeting their needs in the days ahead?

Chapter 7

It's Different for Them: A Look at Age Differences

When you understand what is a normal response for the age of your child, you'll know how to help him or her through the process of grief. The first step is to realize that a child grieves differently from an adult. Instead of experiencing ongoing and intense distress, a child is likely at first to deny death, then grieve intermittently for many years. Other unique features of childhood grief include the following:

- Grief comes out in the middle of everyday life. It can't be predicted.
- A child can put grief aside easier than an adult. One question may be about her grandfather's death; the very next question will be about her doll.
- Grief comes out in brief but intense "episodes."
- Being limited in verbal expression, a child expresses his grief in actions.
- A child often postpones her grief—or at least part of it.
- A child's grief often lasts *throughout* childhood; pieces of it last into adulthood.

In light of these unique qualities of childhood grieving, I'd like to use two different scenarios, involving variously aged children, to help set the stage for what you can anticipate.

SCENARIO: WHEN AN UNCLE SUDDENLY DIES...

Imagine a family with a beloved favorite uncle named Phil. He keeled over suddenly while eating his third bratwurst at the family's annual Fourth of July picnic. Everyone panicked, shouting for help, while two of the brothers threw Phil into a car and rushed him to the hospital. However, there never was a chance to save Uncle Phil. He had suffered a massive heart attack. What effect does this have on the various nieces and nephews?

Jimmy is two and a half years old. He's at the age of helplessness. Uncle Phil had spent a lot of time with Jimmy, so he, too, feels this loss. Not only that, Jimmy feels unprotected because some of the consistency of his life has been taken away.

Mary is four, and she thinks death is temporary and reversible. Uncle Phil is dead today, but he'll be home tomorrow. For her, and others her age, death is similar to taking a trip from which you return. Mary asks her mom, "Can we send Uncle Phil an e-mail?"

John is seven. He knows that when you're dead, you're dead, but he doesn't believe that he himself will die. This is how he's similar to a preschool child: He thinks he's immune. But he wants to know if death is contagious. *Will life still be safe for me?* If John sees Uncle Phil's body, he'll ask question after question, behind which may be a deep concern over his own safety.

1. For a few moments, put yourself into the shoes of Jimmy, Mary, and John. We have an idea of how they are thinking in this grief situation. What *feelings* are they experiencing?

   a. Jimmy's feelings:

   b. Mary's feelings:

   c. John's feelings:

SCENARIO: WHEN A CLASSMATE HAS A TERRIBLE ACCIDENT...

Kaisha was running and playing on the school playground at recess. She never saw the big delivery truck swerving toward her over the sidewalk. The vehicle, driven by a man with a great deal of alcohol in his system, never slowed. Little Kaisha fell under its huge wheels in an instant.

Most of the other children on the playground saw everything that happened, along with Mrs. Harris, the third-grade teaching assistant. She quickly ushered all the children into the gymnasium while school administrators called for an ambulance and the police.

What about the other kids?

Fred, a six-year-old, keeps asking Mrs. Harris questions like these:

"I didn't see Kaisha after she got hit. Was there a lot of blood?"

"What did her head look like?"

"Were her eyes closed?"

You may not want to talk about these things, but the child needs to. Knowing some of the details provides him with a sense of relief.

Justin, an eleven-year-old, also witnessed the accident at the playground. His main question is, "Did her family have any insurance?"

When the child becomes a preadolescent (nine to twelve), he will probably have an adult understanding of death. For him, death is permanent and irreversible. But he will tend to intellectualize his losses and seem to become overly clinical with some of his questions and comments.

2. Once again, jot some of your thoughts about what each child is feeling. Then consider, which of the children seems to represent most closely the feelings your own child may be experiencing these days?

a. Fred's feelings:

b. Justin's feelings:

c. What are your key insights about the effect of a child's age upon how he or she will react to death and/or loss?

DIFFERENT AGES, DIFFERENT RESPONSES

These two scenarios have hinted at some of the characteristics of grief you'll see at various age levels. Now let's get more specific about those qualities by breaking down the age levels in greater detail (but note that some of these have overlapping age *ranges*). Be ready to apply my highly generalized descriptions to the child you know best: yours.

Infant to toddler. The very young express distress when responding to a loss. At this stage, even separation from Mom is felt as a significant loss. If the separation is sudden, the child will express shock and protest. Prolonged separation creates despair and sadness. The child loses interest in toys and activities that are usually pleasurable. Unless a caring individual steps into the vacated role, the infant will become detached from everyone.

Ages two through five. Because they don't understand the significance of the loss, these kids may ask seemingly useless questions again and again and again: "Hasn't he been dead long enough?"

Comprehending concepts takes time, and the idea of death hasn't been fully formed yet in their minds. They may seem bewildered and tend to regress in their behaviors, even becoming demanding and clinging. If what was lost is not returned, expect expressions of anger to increase.

An adult may need to help the children identify, acknowledge, and express feelings of loss. Many adults make the mistake of removing children from familiar surroundings after a family death or trauma. This further undermines their sense of security and raises their anxiety levels.

3. At these very young ages, children are literal and concrete in their thinking. Thus, they can easily be confused by direct or overheard statements. Be a four-year-old, and in the spaces provided, jot down what you think the adult is talking about in the following statements. (The first one is done for you.)

Adult: "Don't pull my leg!"
Child's interpretation: Is somebody hurting you, Dad?

Adult: "That's a bunch of baloney."
Child's interpretation:

Adult: "Keep your shirt on."
Child's interpretation:

Adult: "Don't give up the ship."
Child's interpretation:

Adult: "Hang in there, kid."
Child's interpretation:

Ages three through seven. Children between the ages of three and seven years old engage in *magical thinking.* They believe their own thoughts can influence people and events. For instance, a child who is upset about a parent taking a trip, may wish the car would have a flat tire so the parent won't leave. If the parent is killed in a car crash caused by a blowout, the child feels responsible.

The magical thinking we're talking about is the inaccurate conclusion that a child reaches about a loss experience. Usually, it's that he is responsible for what happened. Thus, he takes on a need to fix it.

A child makes inaccurate conclusions because of her limited cognitive ability. When a child engages in magical thinking, it diverts her from healthy mourning.

4. When you face magical thinking, practice your discernment abilities and respond to the underlying feelings and motives that come through. Following are some examples of magical-thinking statements. Under each, jot one of these words to show what is the underlying emotion to which the adult can respond: fear, anger, sadness, guilt. (The first example is done for you.)

   "I was sick when I kissed Uncle Harry at the picnic. Now Uncle Harry has died."
   Underlying emotion: Guilt

   "A kid in my class at school got run over by a car. He was six years old, but I don't want to be six years old."
   Underlying emotion(s): _____

   "When I'm good, I feel better. If I'm really good all the time, then I'm going to be really happy."
   Underlying emotion(s): _____

   "Mom and Dad got mad at me because I was bad—and then they had a big fight. Now they're getting a divorce."
   Underlying emotion(s): _____

"I can take this light saber and kill the bad man who hurt Jenny. If he comes back, I'll use my dyna-blaster pistol."
Underlying emotion(s): _____

At this age, children don't understand the permanency of death. For them, it's reversible. E.T. came back from the dead. So did Jesus and Lazarus. And so does the coyote in the roadrunner cartoons.

Ages five through eight. Five- through eight-year-olds often feel pressure to be strong and self-reliant. This is brought on by their fear for themselves and concern for other family members. They may become more helpful than usual in order to shut out the pain of their loss and feel more in control.

Early-elementary-age children begin to reason sequentially. Therefore the understanding of death becomes more specific, factual, precise—and more matter of fact than emotional. As they progress, they become more curious about death, funerals, and burials. And they don't see any contradiction in talking about positive results when there's been a death.

5. You are the uncle (or aunt) of seven-year-old Jimmy, and you are sitting next to each other after the funeral. Jimmy turns to you and says, "I know my sister died; I miss her. But Mommy and Daddy have more time for me now." Write several snippets of dialogue below, showing how you would respond to Jimmy's thoughts and feelings.

Your responses to Jimmy's initial statement:

How the dialogue might flow from there:

Jimmy:

You:

Jimmy:

You:

Ages nine through twelve. Children between the ages of nine and twelve years old experience dramatic changes in their thinking processes. They are now developing *conceptual thinking* and *problem-solving skills.*

Toward the end of this stage, they also move from *concrete* to *abstract* thinking. Children who are beginning to think abstractly relate more to real-life people and events than to a fantasy or a make-believe world. They begin to understand the meaning and ramifications of loss. If the loss is a death, they are now able to reflect on the consequences of death, and that's evident in their questions. They may ask:

"What will happen to Frieda now?"

"Who will take care of her grandfather?"

"Will Bill have to move now?"

Even though their thinking is more developed, they do jump to conclusions. They don't always understand what they hear, especially if it's communicated to them in adult terminology. Adults need to communicate clearly to these children, using simple statements, repeating and rephrasing important points of the message.[1]

6. It's important to identify what may inhibit a child's abilities to grieve his losses. Consider the following factors that most often contribute to this problem, and note your thoughts about each in the spaces provided.

a. The parents may be unable to handle and accept their children's expressions of painful experiences. They don't know how to respond. How did you respond the last time?

b. The children may be worried about how the parents are handling the loss; they attempt to protect the adults. Have you seen this in your child? Give an example:

c. The children may be overly concerned with maintaining control and feeling secure. They may be frightened or threatened by the grief. Has this occurred in your family? What were the signs?

d. The parent may not caringly prod, stimulate, and encourage the children to grieve. Do you know what to say? What will you say?

e. In the case of a loved one's death, children may question their role in making it happen. Their misplaced guilt is further enhanced if they have ambivalent feelings toward the loved one. Can you recall this occurring in your life?

———◆———

7. In quietness, review what you've written and learned in this workbook chapter. As further thoughts or ideas come to mind, jot them here:

8. What for you was the most meaningful concept or truth in this chapter? How will you attempt to apply it to your life and/or the life of your children and family?

9. Take some time to hold your children in your thoughts and prayers. Consider what they need from you at the moment. What are some of the ways you can begin meeting their needs in the days ahead?

Chapter 8

Think Their Thoughts

Have you learned to use truthful language about death with your child? When we're not clear as to how a child will think about what happened, we might get a little queasy dealing with the topic at all. Will we just be causing more confusion and pain? That's why too often we want to protect the child with "nice" explanations. Or we choose to believe they can't handle what really happened, so we just clam up.

"We lost him" is a common phrase when someone dies, but to your child he is not dead. Little Jimmy will want to go out and look for the person you lost! If it was an illness, distinguish between a minor and a fatal illness. Your child will learn that other children die, but you can reassure him that it is only when a child is *very* sick, has a terminal illness, or has an accident that he or she dies.

BEST POLICY: THE SIMPLE TRUTH

What you say and how you say it sets the stage for the thinking-and-feeling responses of your child. Therefore, we must courageously force ourselves to tell the truth in ways our children can comprehend. We tell them, "Uncle Jim has gone to sleep for a long, long time." No, he didn't. Uncle Jim has died. Why inject a fear of sleeping into a child's mind?

I've heard so many explanations for death that are not only untrue but damaging. No doubt you've heard some of the "classics" too:

"God wanted your mother to help Him in heaven."

"Your baby brother is a singing angel in heaven now."

"She was too good for this world. God wanted her in heaven."

And we wonder why a child begins to misbehave (he wants to stay here with you, not be whisked away)! It's better to say, "She died because she had a disease called AIDS," or "He died because he was riding his bicycle and ran into a car."

One more reason why telling the truth is so important: Loss heavily impacts children's theological beliefs. What they believe about God (rightly or wrongly) undergoes radical change. We call this a crisis of faith. Questions never before asked now arise. If answers aren't truthful or accurate, the child experiences yet another loss: trust in adults.

1. If you have any fears about telling your child the truth regarding death or loss in the family, write those fears here:

    a. To what degree are your fears hindering clear, simple, and honest communication with your child?

    b. What first step can you take to overcome one of these fears? (Example: Try stating one small, painful truth to your child. Observe whether the child's reaction is one of relief or deeper pain.)

So...How Will You Handle the Funeral?

What happens when it comes time for making the final arrangements? This is where you must be intentional about understanding how your child thinks. The thoughts, feelings, and behaviors of children vary at this time, but this is the key: *They continue to be strongly influenced by the reactions of the surviving family members as well as other adults.*

What opportunities do children need when a relative dies? As you formulate your answer, keep in mind these four pertinent guidelines:

- Children can be given a choice about whether to attend the wake, funeral, or burial.
- Including children in the planning of the funeral has a positive effect.
- Children who are involved want the funeral to reflect the life of the relative.
- Visiting the grave helps children remain connected with the loved one.

2. Get ready for the questions! The problem is that many adults don't know what to expect, are uncomfortable with what they encounter, and struggle with answering the questions streaming from their children, especially since magical thinking in children will likely produce some pretty far-out questions! How would you answer the following?

   What is a casket?
   My response:

   (Other questions to expect: "Can you breathe in a casket? What if they want to get out? How do they go to the bathroom in there?")

   What is cremation?
   My response:

(Other questions to expect: "Does it hurt? Does the body smell? What do they put the ashes in, and what do they do with them?")

What is a funeral?
My response:

(Other questions to expect: "Why do some people cry and some don't at the funeral? Why do some people laugh and some don't at the funeral? If the person is already in heaven, can he hear us at the funeral?")

What is a viewing?
My response:

(Other questions to expect: "Can you touch the body? Does the person look normal? Does she smell?")

Will I have to keep going back to the grave?
My response:

(Other questions to expect: "Billy says we have to go back and visit the grave and put flowers on it. Do I have to go? Uncle Jim is dead. He won't know if we come or not, right?")[1]

Always be clear and as factual as possible, telling the truth about the death and what caused it. When kids ask questions, give them accurate information such as, "Your brother's heart stopped beating, and that is why he died." As I've stressed elsewhere, it's much better to use proper death language, such as "Grandpa died," rather than "Grandpa went to sleep." But be sensitive about how many details you give. If you have no answer to their questions, say so. Let them know, though, that when you do, you will share it with them.

3. It's a good idea to prepare your funeral explanations in advance. Here's a chance for you to think it through. Try fitting the following sample explanation around your family's plans and special traditions:

_____ will be taken from _____, where he died, to the funeral home. At the funeral home _____ will be dressed in clothes that he liked and put into a casket. A casket is a box we use so that when _____ is buried, no dirt will get on him. Because _____'s body isn't working anymore, it won't move or do any of the things it used to do. But it will look like _____ always did.

People will come and visit us and say how sorry they are that _____ died. After _____ days the casket will be closed and taken to the church, where people will say prayers for the family. Then we will go to the cemetery where _____ will be buried in a place that _____ picked out.

If you like, you can come to the funeral home and visit for a while—even go to the cemetery. You could bring something to leave with _____ if you want. That would be nice.

We have to go to the funeral home to make plans, and we'll let you know all about them when we come back. We will be gone _____ hours.

For cremation, use this additional information:

After we leave the funeral home, _____ will be taken to a crematory, a place where his body will be turned into ashes. Then we will take those ashes and _____ (scatter them; keep them in an urn). Since _____'s body doesn't work and doesn't feel anything, being cremated doesn't hurt.

While grieving, our children look to us for hope and encouragement. When they ask us questions, we need to avoid giving them platitudes and, instead, let them know it's all right to ask *why* when bad things happen. We need to admit to them that we don't have all the answers but that we'll get through it together. One mother told her six-year-old, "I know it is a sad time for you. We are all sad and wish things were different. There are many changes happening right now, but in time things will settle down. Someday the pain will go away. It may go away gradually and keep returning again and again, but as we help and love one another, it is going to go away."[2]

When you experience the death of a family member or friend, ask yourself if this is your child's first experience with death. If it is, your child will need your help to understand the loss and sort out his or her feelings about it. Use words and phrases the child can easily understand. It may help to rehearse with someone else what you plan to say.

4. Be especially sensitive to the child's reactions and anticipate the unexpected. For example, one way some children react to a death is to engage in symbolic play. Take some time right now to think about how your child usually plays. Then carefully consider how he or she has changed in type of play or other habits.

   a. My child usually likes to play in these ways:

   b. Some of the patterns or themes I've noticed in my child's day-to-day play are...

   c. Since the loss/death of (name), my child now plays in these ways:

   d.   What patterns or themes, if any, *have changed* since the loss?

Your child's play will give you clues as to what is going on inside. You can then respond appropriately to those thoughts and feelings.

   e.   One way I can respond to my child in the week ahead would be to…

———◆———

As we close this chapter, remember: Your marriage and your other children don't have to be secondary casualties of the original loss. You can take steps to strengthen your marriage and family life, and then you'll have a greater source of strength to draw from as you confront the issues facing you. As your family works, plays, and worships together, you will discover a healing comfort in these relationships. And be sure you allow the other family members to minister to you as you minister to them.

   5.   In quietness, review what you've written and learned in this workbook chapter. As further thoughts or ideas come to mind, jot them down here:

6. What for you was the most meaningful concept or truth in this chapter? How will you attempt to apply it to your life and/or the life of your children and family?

7. Take some time to hold your children in your thoughts and prayers. Consider what they need from you at the moment. What are some of the ways you can begin meeting their needs in the days ahead?

Chapter 9

Feel Their Feelings Too

Assuming you've already learned to mourn your own losses of the past—and are continually involved in that process—you are well qualified to explore what children feel in their crises of loss. Consider, then, a child's emotional reactions to a serious loss such as death. We'll focus specifically on the anger, fear, and guilt that come crashing in...after the shock.

ANCHORED IN ANGER?

Anger affects all of us but baffles children and parents alike. Some children express their anger like heat-seeking missiles. There's no warning. Or your child's anger may be stealthy. Like a submarine attack, it suddenly sneaks into your discussion.

In any case, remember that anger is a warning sign, a clue to underlying attitudes. It may be the first emotion we're aware of, but it is rarely the first emotion we experience in a particular situation. Here's the point: At an early age *many of us learned that anger can divert our attention from these more painful emotions.* So we could speak of at least three causes of anger: hurt, frustration, and fear.

1. Consider each of the cases of childhood anger that follow. What do you think could be going on behind the anger?

    a. Frank, twelve years old, is accused of killing the neighbor's cat. When questioned by his dad, Frank said it was just an accident...and then blurted out,

"Hey, if Mom hadn't taken Rover with her after the divorce, I'd still have a pet of my own!" *Describe what hurt(s) may be underlying Frank's anger:*

b. Sally, three years old, dumped flour and sugar all over the kitchen floor. She proceeded to mix in water and orange juice while pounding the concoction with a wooden spoon. Sally's brother Derrick, a teenager, has been dying of cancer during the past year. Mother had just changed the sheets on Derrick's bed when she walked into the kitchen to discover the mess. *Describe what frustration(s) may be underlying Sally's anger:*

c. The father of six-year-old Julio died in a boating accident last spring. Today, at the public swimming pool, Julio kept running around the pool and pushing other kids into the water. When the lifeguard corralled him, Julio said a curse word and refused to sit in time-out. Also, Julio never got into the water. *Describe what fear(s) may be underlying Julio's anger:*

Children express anger in a variety of ways that you can watch for: stubbornness, half-hearted efforts, forgetfulness, not hearing, laziness. Your child may act confused, pretend she doesn't understand, or be overly clumsy, "accidentally" breaking things on purpose. All of these expressions can be very irritating, but you will know what's going on.

What, specifically, can you do to help your child with anger? For one thing, realize that anger tends to push others away or elicit defensiveness; we're more drawn to the expression of these other emotions. However, when your child displays anger, you could try responding with something along these lines:

"Tell me about your hurt…fear…frustration. I'd like to hear about that."

"It sounds like something is really bothering you. I'm wondering if you're frustrated about something or feeling hurt or perhaps afraid. Could you tell me about it?"

"I'm wondering if, along with your anger, you might be feeling…"

What you're doing is getting at the cause, or source, of the anger: the hurt, frustration, and fear. It's worth a try, right?

FEELING THE FEAR?

Grieving children are often afraid, but they have difficulty actually stating what they're afraid of. Maybe they're too upset or don't have the verbal skills to adequately express themselves. It won't help to try forcing it out of them or shaming them into telling you. Your best approach is patience and continued observation.

You may find it helpful to keep a log of the times your children are afraid. By making comparisons, you can discover a pattern that will help you identify the source of their fears. As with adults, so it is with children: Repeatedly facing our fears is the best method of overcoming them.

2. Counselors often use sentence-completion exercises to help children express their feelings. In the following examples, respond as you think your child would complete the sentences. Later, make time to do the exercise with your child. Finally, in a period of quiet reflection, prayerfully consider how your perceptions differed from your child's reality.[1]

- I feel afraid when…

- I remember a time when I was really afraid. What happened was…

- One thing that really helps when I'm afraid is...

- When I'm afraid, I need my parents to...

- One way I know God is with me is...

- The best thing for me to do when I'm afraid is to...

GOING THROUGH GUILT?

With many childhood losses, children end up feeling guilty. It's difficult to identify all of the sources of guilt, but there seem to be three main reasons children experience guilt when loved ones die:

- "They died because I did something wrong. I misbehaved!"
- "I wanted them dead. I thought it, and it happened."
- "I guess I didn't love them enough."

As an adult, you understand cause and effect better than your child, who may be doing some magical thinking. For example, Jimmy's struggle with regret-guilt is common among children. He would get angry at his brother, Phil, from time to time. He wished Phil would go live with his grandparents. He wanted Phil to leave him alone and quit picking on him.

One day Phil *did* go away. Permanently.

A car ran into Phil's school bus, and Phil died. But Jimmy felt responsible. He began saying things like, "I wish I hadn't..." and "If only I..."

When you hear regret statements, they're usually tied to guilt. If you suspect your child is experiencing guilt, you might ask, "John, do you ever find yourself thinking, 'If only I had...' or 'I wish I could have...'?" Offering such prompts—and then listening carefully—could help your child express his self-tormenting statements.

3. In some rare cases, a child may feel guilty because he actually was the cause of an accidental death or injury. Here is the time to pray for a powerful sense of God's

forgiveness to flow into your child's life. This may take time and much struggle; there are no easy answers or quick cures in such cases. Yet the Bible is clear about what happens when we face our failings and the pain they bring. Do a quick review of the following scriptures, and write down any thoughts and responses that come to mind:

Blessed is he
    whose transgressions are forgiven,
    whose sins are covered.
Blessed is the man
    whose sin the LORD does not count against him
    and in whose spirit is no deceit.

When I kept silent,
    my bones wasted away
    through my groaning all day long.
For day and night
    your hand was heavy upon me;
my strength was sapped
    as in the heat of summer.
Then I acknowledged my sin to you
    and did not cover up my iniquity.
I said, "I will confess
    my transgressions to the Lord"—
and you forgave
    the guilt of my sin. (Psalm 32:1-5)

But Zion said, "The LORD has forsaken me,
   the Lord has forgotten me."

"Can a mother forget the baby at her breast
   and have no compassion on the child she has borne?
Though she may forget,
   I will not forget you!" (Isaiah 49:14-15)

Who is a God like you,
   who pardons sin and forgives the transgression
   of the remnant of his inheritance?
You do not stay angry forever
   but delight to show mercy.
You will again have compassion on us;
   you will tread our sins underfoot
   and hurl all our iniquities into the depths of the sea. (Micah 7:18-19)

For I will forgive their wickedness
   and will remember their sins no more. (Hebrews 8:12)

If God is for us, who can be against us? He who did not spare his own Son, but gave him up for us all—how will he not also, along with him, graciously give us all things? Who will bring any charge against those whom God has chosen? It is God who justifies. Who is he that condemns? Christ Jesus, who died—more than that, who was raised to life—is at the right hand of God and is also interceding for us. (Romans 8:31-34)

If we confess our sins, he is faithful and just and will forgive us our sins and purify us from all unrighteousness....

This then is how we know that we belong to the truth, and how we set our hears at rest in his presence whenever our hearts condemn us. For God is greater than our hearts, and he knows everything.

Dear friends, if our hearts do not condemn us, we have confidence before God and receive from him anything we ask, because we obey his commands and do what pleases him. (1 John 1:9; 3:19-22)

Along with regret-guilt is another form rarely talked about: relief-guilt. Adults and children experience this. Jean's younger sister, Becky, had been sick for five years. Naturally, Becky was the focus of the family's attention. Jean often felt left out—left with the leftovers. When Becky died, Jean was sad...but also quite relieved. After all, she wouldn't have to share her parents anymore, and she would get the attention she'd been wanting. But her relief carried a load of guilt with it. The more relief she felt, the more guilt she felt.

4. If you were Jean's mother, what do you think you'd say to your little girl?

How Can I Encourage the Feelings?

Naturally, you'd like to help your child share his feelings. Let me suggest the following method.

5. Complete the following exercises under anger, guilt, and fear for yourself as a trial run before helping your child through them. As you answer for yourself, think: *What can I expect when working with my child on these exercises?*

Anger:
What is it?
Let's give it a color: _____
Let's give it a sound: _____
Let's give it a smell: _____
What does your body say when you get angry?

What do you look like when you get angry?

Let's draw a picture of anger:

Fear:
What is it?
Let's give it a color: _____
Let's give it a sound: _____

Let's give it a smell: _____

What does your body say when you're afraid?

What do you look like when you're afraid?

Let's draw a picture of fear:

Guilt:

What is it?

Let's give it a color: _____

Let's give it a sound: _____

Let's give it a smell: _____

What does your body say when you feel guilty?

What do you look like when you feel guilty?

Let's draw a picture of guilt:

It may help at this point to have the child read you stories from a book like *Fears, Doubts, Blues and Pouts* by H. Norman Wright and Gary Oliver. (This book can be ordered from Christian Marriage Enrichment by calling 1-800-875-7560.) Using stories or fables is a unique way to help a child discover and understand the cause for a loss in her life. Consider these stories.

The funeral fable. Let your child know you're going to share a story with him. In fact, both of you are going to create a story. For the child who understands death, you could say, "A funeral procession is going down a street, and the people who see it ask, 'Who died?'"

Someone answers, "Oh, it's somebody in the family who lives in this house." "Who is it?"

Now the child continues with the story. If the child is so young that he or she doesn't understand death, say: "Somebody in the family took a trip and went far, far away. In fact, they went so far away they will never come back." (List the members of the family for this child.) An additional question you could ask: "Why would a person go away like this?"

The anxiety fable. "There was a child, and he was talking safely to himself. He said, 'Oh, I'm afraid.' What do you think he was afraid of?" (Additional questions: "What does being afraid do to us?" Why are children afraid? What could we do about this fear?")

The news fable. This is a way to discover both the wishes and fears of a child. "A child comes back home from [school, church, visiting friends], and his mommy says, 'Sit down. I have something to tell you.' What do you think she is going to say? What's the expression on her face? What *don't* you want her to say? What would you *like* her to say?"

The bad dream fable. "Have you ever had a bad dream? Well, this child woke up one morning. He had slept all night, but he was still really, really tired. He said, 'Oh, I had a bad dream.' What was the dream about?"[2]

6. For each of those four fables, answer:
   a. How could I use this fable with my own child?

b. What changes or additions would help the stories be more relevant to my child (or our family loss situation)?

c. What would be a hindrance, or obstacle, to using this story approach with my children?

———◆———

7. In quietness, review what you've written and learned in this workbook chapter. As further thoughts or ideas come to mind, jot them down here:

8. What for you was the most meaningful concept or truth in this chapter? How will you attempt to apply it to your life and/or the life of your children and family?

9. Take some time to hold your children in your thoughts and prayers. Consider what they need from you at the moment. What are some ways you can begin meeting their needs in the days ahead?

Chapter 10

Help Them Get Unstuck

Often I hear parents ask: "How do I know if she's recovering...or if she's *stuck?*"

Sometimes a child can indeed get stuck in the grieving process. What does "stuck" look like? It's called *complicated mourning*, and I'll quickly list some of the signs before delving into one of them more fully:

Denial that doesn't change. Your child won't accept what has happened.

Physical complaints that don't let up. You'll hear: "I have a headache, backache, stomachache, sideache," but even the family doctor can't find any cause for these complaints.

Fear, guilt, or anger that won't subside. These three emotions continue to undermine your child's life.

Withdrawal that's universal. Sometimes a child will withdraw from one family member; now she withdraws from *everyone.*

Personality that's dramatically different. Your child was outgoing but is now constantly withdrawn or once was gracious and encouraging but now is aggressive and sarcastic.

Eating and sleeping that's abnormal. Some children stop eating; others can't seem to stop feeding themselves. This isn't normal—nor is insomnia or constant sleeping.

Use that's abuse. An adolescent may attempt to deaden his pain by using drugs and alcohol as a means of self-medicating.

Regression that's overly dependent. Let's talk more about this one later.

1. Pause here for a moment to picture

    ...the face of your child. What is the level of peace or tension you see?

…the body of your child. What is the level of peace or tension you see?

…the recent behavior of your child. What is the level of peace or tension you see?

What are your insights about whether your child is stuck to some degree in the grieving process?

WATCH FOR UNHEALTHY REGRESSION

Along with the signs of complicated mourning I've listed, watch for regression. It's usually happening when parents are saying things like…

"Quit acting like a baby!"

"Grow up!

"I thought you'd stopped doing that last year!"

Consider a child of ten who wants to return to the security and sense of protection she felt when she was six. She remembers the structure and predictability. Taking on the behavior of those "good old days," she goes back in time.

What can you expect when this occurs? Your child will lean on you in every way, from the physical to the emotional. There's an overdependence. Even the delight of going outside to play can't pry her loose. She may not want you to leave for work or go anywhere that she can't go. If she was nursed or rocked as an infant, this, too, may be requested. You may wake up one night and find your child in bed with you or wrapped in a blanket, asleep, on the floor next to you. The skills your child once mastered now seem to have vanished. You may be asked to tie her shoes, help her dress, or feed her. Don't be alarmed by these responses. They won't last forever.

2. When regressing, your child needs warm emotional support. What you're seeing are symptoms caused by the loss. It's your child saying, "I have needs too." How would you evaluate your present ability to provide such support—especially amid the kinds of behaviors described in the previous paragraphs?

HELP THEM GET UNSTUCK!

Some children get stuck and need a special invitation to share their feelings as well as help learning how to express sorrow. A few sensitive, well-directed questions can often draw them out. If your children still cannot talk, don't force it. Just let them know that you are available and ready to listen when they want to talk.

3. Remember that children express their emotions mostly through actions, symbolic play, and bodily sensations. So think carefully about how your child in particular expresses herself. Complete each of the following sentences with specific details of what you're observing.

   When my child is angry, she...

   When my child is sad, he...

   When my child is frustrated, she...

   When my child is happy, he...

When my child is afraid, she…

When my child experienced the loss/death of (name), he…

Being available may be the most important support you can offer in helping your children get unstuck. Remember, they need affection and a sense of security in order to grieve. Touching them and making eye contact will provide comfort and reassurance. Let your children know it is normal to have ups and downs when grieving. They are not going crazy. Help them break the mourning into manageable pieces so they don't become overwhelmed. Using illustrations and word pictures can help them identify and talk about their feelings.

Following are some more ways you can help "unstick" them.

Give them opportunities for creative expression. Children who have difficulty verbalizing their feelings may find it easier to express them on paper. One creative approach is called Body Tracing. Take a large sheet of butcher paper, and ask your child to lie faceup on it. Then trace your child's body outline with a marker. Now ask your child to get up, and invite him to color the parts of his body that feel sadness, fear, anger, guilt, happiness, or anxiety. You may suggest different colors for different feelings.

Pay attention to how forcefully or gently your child colors a certain area. Does he omit certain areas? Ask your child if he can say the feeling word that goes with the place he colored. If not, that's okay. You may ask him if he would like to tell you about the picture. Listen carefully and encourage him with questions.[1]

4. In preparation for a Body Tracing activity with your child, quickly sketch the outline of your child's body in the space below. Write down your guesses as to what kinds of feelings he is experiencing these days.

Allow your children to respond in their own ways. Don't expect your kids to respond as you do. Initially, they may not seem upset or sad. Young children may even have difficulty remembering the deceased. You may need to help them remember their relationship with the deceased before they can resolve their grief. Showing photos and videos will help, as will reminiscing about times spent together. The important thing is to allow children to progress at their own rates.

Create opportunities for playtime. Play is an important form of expression for children, especially for younger children whose verbal skills are limited. In the safety of play, a child can vent all kinds of feelings. Play helps them regain a feeling of safety and security. It gives them a feeling of power over the effects of loss and allows them to separate themselves from what has happened.[2]

5. You and your child might want to schedule a playtime with boxes—pretend ones. Here's how it works: Imagine yourself in a room full of boxes. Label each box with one of the following emotions. Put the strongest emotion you feel in the biggest box, and then fill the rest of the boxes accordingly.

   loneliness
   guilt
   anger/depression/sadness
   unforgiveness
   fear/worry
   other emotions you might be feeling:

   Imagine that the biggest box contains the most painful emotion you feel. The boxes graduate in size, according to the intensity of feelings. The emotion in the biggest box may change from day to day. (If you are not sure where to start, just choose one emotion and start there.) Now imagine that you push the smaller boxes aside, take the larger box, and open the lid. What is the emotion telling you?

Encourage children to continue their normal routines. It helps if children continue certain family routines. Routines provide security, letting them know there are certain constants in their lives, things they can rely on to stay the same.

6. In the midst of grief, are you allowing your children to live a normal life? Following is a partial checklist of normal childhood activities. Place a check mark next to activities you would like to add (or add *back*) to the routine of your child's life, even while feeling a loss.

    ___ Playing catch on the front lawn
    ___ Having friends come for a sleepover
    ___ Laughing and giggling for silly reasons
    ___ Praying together
    ___ Reading together
    ___ Lying in bed together
    ___ Taking day trips to special places
    ___ Hugging and kissing
    ___ Your idea: _____
    ___ Your idea: _____
    ___ Your idea: _____
    ___ Your idea: _____
    ___ Your idea: _____
    ___ Your idea: _____

BE READY TO BE FRUSTRATED

Even when our expectations seem thoroughly reasonable and appropriate, we may feel as if our children still aren't "doing it right" for us. Then our own frustration can set in. As our children talk to us about a death, we may find ourselves frustrated for several reasons. Here are three common reasons:

Your child may talk as though the person (or pet) is still alive. So you will need to remind him that the person is dead. And you might need to do this repeatedly. Naturally, what he asks or talks about could activate some of your own pain. You may wish he'd just keep quiet for a while!

But be clear about this: A grieving child will often try to re-create the former situation. It's his form of denial, or protest, and it can take various forms. For example, he may act as if nothing out of the ordinary has happened. In fact, at first many children respond in this fashion. It's normal. It's their Novocain. It's better than pain. It's their way of saying, "No. You're wrong. It didn't happen."

7. Think about the days ahead if/when your child begins talking about your loved one as though he or she is still alive.

   a. How will you likely react?

   b. How can you prepare yourself to respond with a little more patience or gentleness?

   c. What words, phrases, or actions come to mind as things you'd *like* to say or do?

Your child may keep searching, searching, searching. Kids in grief may try to recover the lost loved one. They know it's not going to work, but they keep trying. This is particularly the case when loved ones are "lost"—missing in action, kidnapped, drowned at sea, or for some other reason the body is missing. Now the challenge becomes, can this loss be reversed? They think, *Maybe it's not really permanent after all!*

Your child will need to keep revisiting and regrieving. Even if you help your child through a difficult loss and you think he's worked through his grief, he will still need to revisit his grief years later. A friend shared with me that her son was nine when his three-year-old brother died after several months of severe medical problems. His mother took him to a counselor who worked with him for some time. The counselor said he appeared to be doing all right at the time but that somewhere between the ages of fifteen and twenty-two he would possibly be affected by this loss again and need to regrieve. And at twenty that's exactly what occurred.

8. Regrieving often occurs as a child enters her next stage of development. Or it may occur during special days on the family calendar—holidays, anniversaries (for example, of the birth or death of the loved one), or gatherings. Note three dates when you think your child might be powerfully affected, once again, by her grief.

    The next possible date: _____. Why?

    The next possible date: _____. Why?

    The next possible date: _____. Why?

9. In quietness, review what you've written and learned in this workbook chapter. As further thoughts or ideas come to mind, jot them down here:

10. What for you was the most meaningful concept or truth in this chapter? How will you attempt to apply it to your life and/or the life of your children and family?

11. Take some time to hold your children in your thoughts and prayers. Consider what they need from you at the moment. What are some ways you can begin meeting their needs in the days ahead?

Chapter 11

Depression: When Feelings Get "Stuffed"

When we are overcome by emotions, we may call it depression or sadness. It's a feeling of numbness, like a big bunch of emotions that makes our heart feel heavy.

We need to find our way through the numbness of depression. Just as when we go to a theme park, we get a map and decide on a starting point, so in working our way through depression, we start by identifying our feelings.

1. Think about the biblical prophet Elijah for a moment. He was one of the great prophets and a mighty man of God. In 1 Kings 19:3-5 we find this story about him:

   > Elijah was afraid and ran for his life. When he came to Beersheba in Judah, he left his servant there, while he himself went a day's journey into the desert. He came to a broom tree, sat down under it and prayed that he might die. "I have had enough, LORD," he said. "Take my life; I am no better than my ancestors." Then he lay down under the tree and fell asleep.

   Elijah faced depression. What did you notice about how he felt in this story? Answer the questions that follow.

____ He was afraid. Why?

____ He ran. What did this do for him?

____ He was overwhelmed. What does this mean to you?

____ He lay down, physically worn out. When do you feel this way?

____ He isolated himself. When do you feel isolated?

____ He felt self-pity. Have you ever felt sorry for yourself? When? How do you behave when you feel sorry for yourself?

What about children? Can they experience what Elijah did—and any adult does—in depression? Actually, they can become depressed for numerous reasons, often because of a loss. Sudden loss is particularly hard on children, leaving them feeling out of control and floundering. On the other hand, a gradual loss that can be prepared for is easier for children to manage.

The important thing for parents to understand is the difference between a healthy sadness and an unhealthy depression. The feeling of sadness is less intense than that of depression; it doesn't last as long, nor does it interfere with day-to-day functioning. Depression causes us to function at 50 percent of normal. It affects diet and sleeping patterns. It is often the result of unexpressed anger—the great energy of frustration turned inward rather than directed at problem solving.

2. Spend some minutes in silence, imagining yourself as a depressed child. (If you were, indeed, depressed as a child, then go back in your memory to your real history.) Think:

   a. What is my body language saying much of the time? What does my face look like? What about my eyes?

   b. How well am I sleeping? How well am I eating?

What Are the Signs of Depression?

Here's a composite of the depressed child—a depressive Top Ten List, if you will. Your child probably won't display all of these symptoms, but be on the lookout for several being displayed together.

1. Sadness and indifference
2. Withdrawal and inhibition
3. Physical complaints
4. Sense of rejection
5. Down on self with negative talk
6. Frustration and irritability
7. Silly facade—masking despair with clowning
8. Up-and-down moods
9. Being the problem—acting like the family's problem child
10. Aggression or passive aggression

c. What am I angry or frustrated about? How have I expressed this anger—or not?

d. What are my adult insights about the effects of anger and frustration that get turned inward?

Many children experience depression because they're having difficulties dealing with people. The strongest need a child has is to belong, to be part of a family and social group. Children who are having problems developing positive relationships are in crisis and can become depressed. Again, they've experienced a loss.

3. A depression-prone child can interpret a parent's response as a reinforcement of his negative worth. See, for example, the parental responses that follow. Think how the child might interpret them, and jot down some notes. (The first three are done for you.)

- Parents focusing on negative or upsetting behavior
  Child's interpretation: "Everyone expects me to be bad."

- Parents' failure to keep promises
  Child's interpretation: "No one cares if I'm disappointed."

- Frequent criticism
  Child's interpretation: "I can't do anything right."

- Lack of individual attention from parent
  Child's interpretation:

- Harsh or angry words from parents
  Child's interpretation:

- Parents' failure to acknowledge accomplishments
  Child's interpretation:

Over time, continuous negative experiences like these contribute to feelings of low self-worth, which lead to depressed feelings.[1]

How You Can Help Your Depressed Child

Review the list of possible signs of depression on page 106. If you notice some of these signs in your child, don't be discouraged. There are things you can do to help your child through this difficult time. For one thing, realize that certain physical problems can cause depressed feelings, so consult with your physician.

Beyond this, you'll want to watch your child's diet, keep him or her busy, give support, and make family adjustments as needed. Remember that your depressed child is a hurting child who isn't feeling the love of God; anything you can do to help reconstruct your child's self-esteem will be beneficial. Obviously, you'll never tease or belittle your child for a lack of self-confidence at this time. And, as shocking as it may be to consider, any suspicions of suicide should be taken seriously. A child or adolescent who expresses utter hopelessness for the future may be at risk. Stay alert.

As your child moves through the dark valley of depression, there are two special helping skills you'll work on as a parent. Let's take a look.

Skill #1: Learn to Answer Emotion with Emotion

Most of us parents have a difficult time coming up with what to say. Depression isn't an everyday occurrence, so it stretches our ability to say something helpful. As you develop your feelings vocabulary, a key step is to learn to *answer emotion with emotion*. This is a form of empathizing.

The difference may seem quite subtle, but remember that sympathy only reinforces someone's feelings of hopelessness. Statements such as "It's awful that you're depressed" tend to encourage helplessness and low self-esteem. Instead, empathize; let the child know you've had similar experiences and that these feelings will pass. Help is available.

4. Here are some examples of what answering with emotion looks and sounds like. It involves trying to name as closely as possible what the child is truly feeling. Study the first two scenarios, and then try your hand at developing empathetic responses in the remaining three scenarios.

   Scenario: Your daughter has just discovered that all her friends are attending a popular girl's party; she has received no invitation.
   Possible parental response: "I can see how disappointed you are that you weren't invited to the party. It must feel like a lump in your throat right now."

   Scenario: Your quarterbacking son came down with the flu on the day of the big game.
   Possible parental response: "I can appreciate that you're upset about missing the game. I know that's frustrating you…and probably causing a lot of tension in your body, huh?"

   Scenario: Your nine-year-old son, who is sulking in the corner of the living room, remembers how his recently deceased dad used to take him fishing on Saturday mornings.
   Your possible response:

   Scenario: Your daughter kicks the wastebasket and yells, "If you and Dad had taken Fido to the vet more often, he never would have died!"
   Your possible response:

Scenario: Three days after the funeral for his big brother, your eleven-year-old son starts being overly polite and oh so helpful, acting like "a little adult." He seems to have a grin constantly pasted on his face.

Your possible response:

SKILL #2: LEARN TO HELP YOUR CHILD EXPRESS FEELINGS

Keep in mind that depression robs people of the ability to govern their thinking and emotions. If your depressed child just stares, ignores greetings, or turns away from you, remember that he doesn't *want* to act that way. He's not trying to punish you. A severely depressed child can't control himself any more than you could walk a straight line after twirling around twenty times. Your help is needed here!

When your child does begin to talk about his or her feelings, follow these important guidelines:

- Understand what is being said from your child's point of view. His interpretation of matters (which might be considerably different from yours) is important since his beliefs will largely determine what he does in the future.

- Be sure your nonverbal expressions indicate a genuine interest in what your child is saying. Avoid anything that might distract you from focusing directly on your child. Lean down to his or her level, or sit on the floor.

- Use gentle, open-ended questions to gather information from your child. Avoid implying wrongdoing or guilt by your tone.[2]

5. Do you take care to make your questions open-ended when possible? It means that you let your child set the agenda of the conversation. You aren't directing him to give you a "right" answer. He is free to respond authentically. In the following, practice turning a yes-or-no question into an open-ended one. (The first two are done as examples.)

- Are you mad because Dad left us?
  An open-ended version: "What are your feelings these days about our family situation?"

- Did you break Sally's toy because you were mad at me?
  An open-ended version: "I'm wondering how Sally's toy got broken…"

- "Didn't you stop to think before yelling at your teacher?"
  An open-ended version:

- "Are you going to eat your supper or not?"
  An open-ended version:

The point is this: With our questions we can subtly *accuse* behaviors or graciously *invite* feelings. Which approach will you choose with your child?

———◆———

Let's close this chapter with what I call the Capable Kid Test. It's a way to help parents evaluate how well their children are responding to anger. We know that stuffed anger can lead to depression, so take a moment to go through the following three steps to see what might be happening with your child.

Step 1: Think of a situation in which your child has experienced anger. It could be sharing a room or a bike with a sibling, having a favorite weekend outing canceled, flunking a test, not making the school team or play, being shunned by friends, or being embarrassed.

Step 2: Think about how your child reacted and whether it was her typical response to that type of situation.

Step 3: Choose one statement from the following list that best describes your child's reactions. Put a check mark in front of the one that strikes you as accurate.

_____ 1. "I never get what I want. Nobody cares about me." (She may become belligerent and verbally abusive.)

_____ 2. He starts going through a list of people to blame.

_____ 3. "Things like this always happen to me. I guess I deserve it."

_____ 4. "Wow, that really hurt!" Then a few seconds later, she says (or thinks), "I'm going to tell him how that felt and ask him not to do that again."

_____ 5. "I shouldn't be surprised. I knew something crummy would happen." (He then becomes withdrawn and preoccupied.)

_____ 6. "That really makes me angry. But maybe I was unkind. I wonder if there is anything I can do about it now."

_____ 7. "That's not fair! It's just not fair. I never get what I want." (She then begins a temper tantrum.)

_____ 8. He doesn't visibly react and pretends everything is normal, but he withdraws, won't talk about it, and tends to isolate himself.

Step 4: Now find the description of your child as indicated. (Remember, the description you select should be your child's *typical* way of responding.) This will clarify for you your child's level of ability to handle stress.

Evaluation:

#4 or #6: Either of these responses indicates a capable person. These children handle stress well, will express disappointment or anger, and then quickly figure out what to do about it. They will feel disappointed rather than greatly upset, and that disappointment will only last a few minutes.

#1, #2, or #7: These children are slightly vulnerable. They have upset reactions, but they don't last long. They soon calm down, become less preoccupied with themselves, and begin to find ways of handling the problem. They need to learn some new ways of coping to become less reactive.

#3, #5, or #8: These children are especially vulnerable. Their responses usually last more than twenty-four hours, and symptoms of being vulnerable are evident in their lives.

6. In quietness, review what you've written and learned in this workbook chapter. As further thoughts or ideas come to mind, note them here:

7. What for you was the most meaningful concept or truth in this chapter? How will you attempt to apply it to your life and/or the life of your children and family?

8. Take some time to hold your children in your thoughts and prayers. Consider what they need from you at the moment. What are some ways you can begin meeting their needs in the days ahead?

Chapter 12

Divorce: A Never-Ending Grief

Newsweek magazine has estimated that 45 percent of all children will live with only one parent at some time before they are eighteen years old. Twelve million children under the age of eighteen now have parents who are divorced. Your family may be intact, but your child will have many friends who come from divorced homes. Since they may look to you as a model of an intact family, you may end up ministering to these children. So you need to be aware of the effect of divorce upon their lives.

WHAT IS DIVORCE LIKE FOR A CHILD?

A child certainly doesn't want a divorce. He is like a bystander caught in a flood, swept away by the current, having to drift with the flow. And a child caught in a divorce experiences multiple losses. These can include not only the loss of one of the parents but also the loss of a home, neighborhood, school friends, the family standard of living, family outings, family holiday get-togethers, and so on. Other losses might include:

- The loss of the expectation that "my family will be together forever"
- The loss of trust: "If I can't depend on my parents, who can I depend on?"
- The loss of the familiar, the routine, and the safe
- The possible loss of frequent access to a set of grandparents as well as the addition of a new set (with a remarriage)
- The loss of part of their childhood

1. Have you ever wondered what it would be like to learn, as a child, that your parents were divorcing and then, in this panic, to begin telling your friends? Spend some quiet moments thinking it through. What are (or were) some of the fears and anxieties you would have (or did have)?

When there is the loss of a parent, there also may be a loss of hope for the future. An uncertainty worms its way into the child's mind; she can feel out of control to a greater extent than ever before. The stable parents upon whom she depended are no longer that solid rock. This may occur in a practical area such as finances. If a divorced father has promised to take care of the family through his monthly payments, what must a child feel when payments become irregular and eventually cease?

Divorce affects children in different ways, depending upon the age of the child. Let's look closer.

Ages three to six. Young children experience deeper fears, and the routine separations of life become traumatic. A parent going shopping or the child's leaving for school is now a stressful experience. Children tend to regress to earlier behavior and become more passive and dependent. More and more they ask "what's that?" questions, which is their effort to overcome the disorganization of crisis.

Many in this age group will regress. They may refuse to feed themselves, and some even revert to a need for diapers. The child can create wild and imaginative fantasies in his mind, because he is puzzled by what's happening to him. He's bewildered. Play doesn't have the same sense of fun.

2. If your child is between ages three and six, jot down some notes about what you are observing in him lately... ·

    a. Related to fear levels:

b. Related to signs of stress:

c. Related to signs of regression:

d. Other observations:

Ages six to eight. A child in this age group has his own set of reactions. Sadness is there, but his sense of responsibility for the parents' breakup becomes stronger. He has deep feelings of loss. He is afraid of being abandoned and sometimes even of starving. He yearns for the parent who has left. Many are convinced their parent has rejected them.

Separation anxieties begin to emerge. A four-year-old who looked forward to her nursery school playground before the divorce now clings to her mother and cries, refusing to leave. Her six-year-old brother used to go to bed at night happily. Now he avoids bedtime, making one request after another. It's water, bathroom, or…protection from monsters. Actually, he wants to see his mother. Baby-sitters don't like to come to this home anymore. Too many temper tantrums!

3. If your child is between ages six and eight, make some notes about what you have observed in her lately…

a. Related to feeling responsible for the breakup:

b. Related to fears of abandonment:

c. Related to separation anxieties:

d. Other observations:

Ages eight to twelve. Preadolescent children usually experience anger as their main emotional response. This anger is directed toward the parent they feel is responsible for the family breakup, and this could be the custodial parent. They're prone to take sides. But anger, instead of coming out directly at the parent, may be directed at peers. Thus these kids may alienate potential friends at the time when they most need them. Their self-image is shaken. Sometimes they throw themselves into what they are doing with great intensity as their way of handling the disruption of their lives. For about half of the children in this group, school performance drops markedly.

This is a time of conscience development, and the divorce may have a shattering effect upon that process. Watch closely for psychosomatic illnesses at this stage.

4. If your child is between ages eight and twelve, jot down some notes about what you are observing in him lately...

   a. Related to anger—expressed or masked:

   b. Related to self-image:

c. Related to friends and school performance:

d. Related to psychosomatic complaints:

e. Other observations:

In all the turmoil, the child seems to have two major concerns. First, she dreams of her parents reconciling. If this were to happen, all her problems would end. She believes, in spite of previous problems, that the family was better off when both parents were there. She may have witnessed all the conflict, but she's usually willing to endure it to have an intact family. After all, this is the only family she knows.

Her second concern revolves around herself: *What's going to happen to me?* She's afraid the custodial parent will abandon her. One parent has already left her, so why shouldn't the other eventually do the same?

REQUIRED: PASSING THROUGH THE EMOTIONAL STAGES

Whether a child's home is quiet and peaceful or filled with visible conflict, the child rarely expects a divorce. He may not like the conflict but hopes it will settle down eventually. Discovering the impending divorce shocks the child's system. All the mixed feelings come crashing in.

The child passes through some fairly well-defined emotional stages as he struggles to understand and deal with the divorce. These stages are normal, and they cannot be avoided or bypassed. *A child needs to pass through these stages in order to produce positive growth and minimize the negative effects.*

Stage #1: Fear and anxiety. The child stares into the mist of an unknown future. A home and family with two parents was once the child's source of stability. That family now shatters.

Stage #2: Abandonment and rejection. The child may know at one level that he will not be rejected or abandoned, but he is still concerned that it might happen. A younger child finds it hard to distinguish between the parents' leaving one another and their leaving *him.* And he may focus on this. This stage may be perpetuated by unkept promises on the part of the parent who leaves.

Stage #3: Aloneness and sadness. As the family structure changes and settles down, the reality of what has occurred begins to settle in. A child feels this stage with a pain in the stomach and a tightness in the chest. This is a time for depression, and regular activities tend to be neglected. Many children do a lot of thinking, which is usually wishful daydreaming.

Stage #4: Frustration and anger. Children whose parents divorce or separate are angry children. This is a natural response to the frustration they feel. In addition, they have seen angry and upset parents; the child begins to emulate this modeled behavior. Anger may continue to be the pattern for many years and may carry over into many relationships.

The anger may not show itself directly though. It may be suppressed or masked. So be on the lookout for the signs of indirect expression. Sarcasm and resistance are fairly easy to spot, but other manifestations may occur in physical complaints such as asthma, vomiting, insomnia, and stomachaches. The child's anger may be expressed through a negative perspective on life, irritability, withdrawal, self-isolation, and resistance to school chores—or whatever the child wants to resist.

It's essential to accept the normalcy of the child's anger, no matter how it's displayed. Encourage the child to talk it out but not to act it out in uncontrolled rage.

5. Think carefully about the implications of these first four stages for your child and family:

a. Why would it be essential for your child to pass through each one?

b. In practical terms, what will this look like for him or her?

c. What effects will experiencing these stages likely have on your family as a whole? (Be specific.)

Stage #5: Rejection and resentment. Eventually the child's anger moves into rejection and resentment. The child is not over his angry feelings but is now attempting to create some emotional distance between himself and his parent. This is a protective device. Pouting can be one form of rejection, as can "the silent treatment." The child won't respond to suggestions or commands and often "forgets" to follow through with what he's supposed to do. He becomes hypercritical.[1]

This behavior is actually what psychologists call *reaction formation.* Paradoxically, as a child pushes a parent away, he really wants to be close to the parent. He shouts hateful statements and yet wants to be loving. He is just trying to protect himself from rejection, so he rejects others first.

Stage #6: Reestablishment of trust. The final stage in the process of dealing with divorce is the reestablishment of trust. It is difficult to say how long this will take, as it varies with each situation and child and can range from months to years.

6. Related to stages #5 and #6, consider:

a. How willing are you to weather the storm of normal expressions of resentment in your child? How prepared are you for this?

b. How patient are you willing to be in order to let the reestablishment of trust happen in its own appropriate time?

———◆———

If you're concerned about the effects of divorce on your child, don't neglect the child's feelings. Each day give him some time to discuss what he is experiencing and feeling. Also determine to continue living in the same home and neighborhood, keeping things the same as much as possible. In addition, guide a child in selecting some task he can accomplish. This will help him overcome a feeling of helplessness.

In the midst of the painful process, convey the assurance that even though Mom and Dad will be working through their own struggles, *both* of them will be taking care of him. Finally, make sure your child knows that, though parents are imperfect, he has a heavenly Parent who will never fail him—the One who is always there for him.

7. In quietness, review what you've written and learned in this workbook chapter. As further thoughts or ideas come to mind, note them here:

8. What for you was the most meaningful concept or truth in this chapter? How will you attempt to apply it to your life and/or the life of your children and family?

9. Take some time to hold your children in your thoughts and prayers. Consider what they need from you at the moment. What are some ways you can begin meeting their needs in the days ahead?

Chapter 13

Trauma: It Shouldn't Happen to a Child

It is not a harmless phenomenon. To children, a trauma is a wound, an ongoing, festering sore that strikes frightening messages into their souls:

Your world is no longer safe.

Your world is no longer kind.

Your world is no longer predictable.

Your world is no longer trustworthy.

Trauma is a condition characterized by the phrase "I just can't seem to get over it." And the saddest thing is to see it in a child. All of us parents pray that it won't happen in our family.

Know These Three *B*s of Trauma

Trauma is more than a state of crisis. It is a normal reaction to abnormal events that overwhelm a person's ability to adapt to life. Trauma makes you feel powerless. It's overwhelming for adults and life shattering for children. If you had the ability to scan little Timmy when he's experienced a trauma, what would you see?

What's happening in his BRAIN. Timmy's thinking process has been distorted. He will experience confusion, a distortion of time, difficulties in solving problems and in figuring out what's best to do next.

Hypersensitivity can actually become wired into basic brain chemistry and bodily functions. In subtle ways the child's brain goes on alert. It's in a "prevent trauma" mode. And after enough chronic experiences, this arousal state becomes a "trait." The child's brain organizes around the overactivated systems to make sure the child survives. Other skills are sacrificed by their defensive posture. It's not a pleasant way to live.[1]

What's happening in his BODY. Timmy's body is out of sync. His heart is probably pounding. He's got nausea, cramps, sweating, headaches, and even muffled hearing. Emotionally, he's riding a roller coaster. He's irritable, afraid, anxious, frustrated, and angry.

Since Timmy's alarm system is stuck, he's hyperaroused. He could suffer from high blood pressure, rapid heart rate or irregular heartbeat, slightly elevated temperature, and constant anxiety. He may go through his life with his alarm button on alert, constantly on the watch for any possible threat.

What's happening in his BEHAVIOR. The bottom line is that if Timmy has experienced a trauma, whether an accident, death, divorce, abuse, or whatever it might be, his parents ought to expect extremes of behavior—either overresponding or underresponding.

Either way, Timmy's behavior is off. He's probably slower in what he does, wanders aimlessly, is dejected, has difficulty remembering, could be hysterical, out of control, and hyper.[2]

1. Trauma creates stress in your child. But how good are you at picking up childhood stress signals? Take some time to review your child's behavior and complaints during the past two or three weeks, and rate the following questions using this scale:

   1 = My child experiences this SOMETIMES (perhaps once a month).
   2 = My child experiences this OFTEN (between once a month and once a week).
   3 = My child experiences this FREQUENTLY (more than once a week).

   ____ Complains of headaches, backaches, or general muscle pains or stiffness.

___ Reports stomach pains, digestive problems, cramps, or diarrhea.

___ Has cold hands or feet, sweaty palms, or increased perspiration.

___ Has a shaky voice, trembles and shakes, displays nervous tics, or grinds and clenches his or her teeth.

___ Gets sores in the mouth, skin rashes, or low-grade infections like the flu.

___ Reports irregular heartbeats, skipped beats, thumping in the chest, or a racing heart.

___ Is restless, unstable, and feels "blue" or low.

___ Is angry and defiant and wants to break things.

___ Has crying spells, and I have difficulty stopping them.

___ Overeats, especially sweet things.

___ Seems to have difficulty concentrating on homework assignments.

___ Reacts very intensely (with angry shouting) whenever he or she is frustrated.

___ Complains of a lot of pain in many places of the body.

___ Seems anxious, fidgety, and restless, and tends to worry a lot.

___ Has little energy and has difficulty getting started on a project.

___ Total Score

How to Rate Your Child's Score

0–5: Remarkably low in stress or handles stressful situations extremely well.

6–12: Showing minor signs of stress. While it is nothing to be concerned about, some attention to stress control may be warranted.

13–20: Beginning to show signs of moderate stress. Some attention should be given to how your child copes with stress.

21–30: Showing significant signs of stress. You should give urgent attention to helping him or her reduce stress levels.

Over 30: Appears to be experiencing very high stress levels. You should do everything possible to eliminate stressful situations until your child can learn to cope. You may want to consider getting professional help.

WHAT ARE SOME AGE-CHARACTERISTIC RESPONSES?

You're reading this book out of concern for your child. So, as I've done in previous chapters, I'd like to break down the childhood responses and reactions by age groups. This is because children of differing ages are in different stages of cognitive and emotional development when they're traumatized. The very nature of brain development causes them to respond in age-related ways. Therefore, we need to know what to expect at certain ages. The following are characteristics of children who have experienced trauma. These posttraumatic stress disorder symptoms are unique to children.

Children under four years old. They tend to "forget" their trauma experiences (consciously, at least for a period of time), although a few may remember from the beginning. Those over this age do remember and tend to remember the experiences vividly, whereas adults often tend to deny reality or repress their memories. Briefly, here are the prominent characteristics:

- Most of these kids don't experience the psychic numbing common to adults. But if it's parental abuse, they do.
- Most don't experience intrusive and disruptive visual flashbacks.
- School performance usually isn't impacted in acute trauma for as long a time as adults' work performance is impacted.
- Play and reenactment increases in frequency. And with a child you will find frequent time distortions.[3]

2. Carefully go over the previous descriptions in light of your own child's experience. Then consider:

    a. What does it mean that children tend to "forget" their trauma experiences? What do you think are the practical implications of this for a child under four years old?

b. If you know that your child under four has experienced abuse or some other trauma, what specific signs will you watch for?

Children of preschool or kindergarten age. Here are the most likely posttraumatic behaviors you'll observe:

- ***Withdrawal.*** This is common, since children react to a trauma with a generalized response of distrust.
- ***Denial.*** This to be expected, including denial of the facts and of memories of the event. They may avoid certain issues or ignore certain people. Distortions are common. Some children embellish the truth or develop gaps in what they remember.
- ***Anxious attachments.*** These can include clinging, whining, not letting go of parents or favorite possessions, and throwing tantrums more frequently. Attachment adjustments during this stage are somewhat common.
- ***Fears.*** These could include being afraid of new situations, specific objects, strangers, males, or being restricted or confined. Such fears could occur at home, on the playground, or in the classroom.

3. As you review these descriptions, consider how you normally react to such behaviors—and how you'd *like* to respond in the future.

a. When my child *withdraws,* I usually…

What I'd like to do instead:

b. When my child *denies* or forgets the facts, I usually…

What I'd like to do instead:

c. When my child *clings* or whines or acts up, I usually…

What I'd like to do instead:

d. When my child expresses significant *fear*, I usually…

What I'd like to do instead:

Younger school-age children. Everything mentioned about preschool children could emerge during this stage as well. But there are some additional posttraumatic characteristics.

- *Performance decline.* Things go downhill in schoolwork, sports, hobbies, music. If this occurs, it could be because the child is acting out or because he is preoccupied with what transpired in his life.
- *Compensatory behavior.* Your child begins trying to compensate for the event itself or the results. There's a purpose to this response, whether he is aware of it

or not. It's his attempt to deny what occurred, to reverse it, or to gain some control or retribution. This could occur through fantasy, playing the event out with others (with a different ending), or talking it out with others.

- *Obsessive talking.* You may end up with what some parents call a chatterbox. Your child talks nonstop.

- *Inappropriate expressions.* This is a common response, even with adults, since in trauma there is a separation or disconnection of the functioning of the left and right sides of the brain. Sometimes a person experiences a flood of feelings (the right side of the brain), but she has no narrative from the left side to explain those feelings. Or the actual events and story may be quite vivid, but there's no emotion at this time.

- *Repetitive reenactments.* A child of this age plays differently from your preschooler. So expect more reenactments of the event in his play and great detail. They don't necessarily help the child in his recovery, but it's another means of expression.

   What do children do when they play a compensatory or reenactment game? They may kill the perpetrator, and if you walk in on this scenario, don't put a stop to it. It's purposeful. Their play may involve acting as if life were normal, as it used to be. Or their play theme may revolve around undoing the damage.

4. Of these five characteristics, which do you think would be the most difficult for an adult to handle? Why?

What kinds of strategies—for meeting the child's needs—would you recommend in each case?

Older children and adolescents. Adolescents, and those on the verge of this stage, tend to act out their distress when they have experienced a trauma. Often their acting out is purposeless and destructive. They're less apt to turn to you as a parent for help; instead, they'll turn to their peers. In addition, you may encounter self-isolation, decreased self-esteem, and displaced anger that misses the appropriate target.

Sometimes traumatized adolescents simply begin acting like adults—"too old, too fast!" They take on adult responsibilities too soon, and there's very little joy in their lives.

5. How can you as a parent help at a time of trauma—during and after? Children and adolescents themselves have identified what they need as well as what they *don't* need in a trauma or crisis. Following is a list of what they've said worked for them. Check the one you think you are doing best. Place a star next to the one or two you would like to improve upon.

   My mom or dad...
   ___ allowed me to talk
   ___ showed warmth and acceptance
   ___ listened well
   ___ respected my privacy
   ___ showed patience
   ___ came through in the past
   ___ showed understanding
   ___ made helpful suggestions
   ___ was there when I needed her/him

6. In quietness, review what you've written and learned in this workbook chapter. As further thoughts or ideas come to mind, jot them down here:

7. What for you was the most meaningful concept or truth in this chapter? How will you attempt to apply it to your life and/or the life of your children and family?

8. Take some time to hold your children in your thoughts and prayers. Consider what they need from you at the moment. What are some ways you can begin meeting their needs in the days ahead?

———◆———

As you come to the end of this workbook, I hope you have grown in awareness and appreciation of the important role of loss in your life and in your child's life. We might even say that there is no such thing as growth—especially *spiritual* growth—without the emptying that comes with loss. I'd like to leave you with that thought as you get ready to face the challenging days ahead with your family. Loss is not the enemy. It is a painful event, and it is always unwanted. But it is also a heavenly calling, as we take up the hard work of grieving.

Come to me, all you who are weary and burdened,
and I will give you rest.
Take my yoke upon you and learn from me,
for I am gentle and humble in heart,
and you will find rest for your souls.
Matthew 11:28-29

Blessed are those who mourn,
for they will be comforted.
Matthew 5:4

Notes

Introduction: When Loss Comes Calling

1. J. William Worden, *Grief Counseling and Grief Therapy: A Handbook for the Mental Health Practitioner* (New York: Springer Publishing, 1982), 10-17.

Chapter 1: Looking Loss in the Eye

1. Martha Wakenshaw, *Caring for Your Grieving Child* (Oakland, Calif.: New Harbinger, 2002), 38-9, adapted.

Chapter 2: Face the Hurt or Try to Protect?

1. John W. James and Russell Friedman with Leslie Landon Matthews, *When Children Grieve: For Adults to Help Children Deal with Death, Divorce, Pet Loss, Moving, and Other Losses* (New York: HarperCollins, 2001), 9.
2. John M. Gottman with Joan DeClaire, *The Heart of Parenting: How to Raise an Emotionally Intelligent Child* (New York: Simon & Schuster, 1997), 52, adapted.

Chapter 4: Sickness...and All Its Big Questions

1. Phyllis Rolfe Silverman, *Never Too Young to Know: Death in Children's Lives* (New York: Oxford University Press, 2000), 115.
2. Joanne M. Hilden and Daniel R. Tobin with Karen Lindsey, *Shelter from the Storm: Caring for a Child with a Life-Threatening Condition* (Cambridge, Mass.: Perseus, 2003), adapted. See introduction and chapters 1-3.
3. Hilden and Tobin, *Shelter from the Storm,* 73-4, adapted.

Chapter 5: In the Family "Machine"—Each Part Affected!

1. Therese A. Rando, *Grieving: How to Go On Living When Someone You Love Dies* (Lexington, Mass.: Lexington Books, 1988), 178-9, adapted.

Chapter 6: The Grieving Family: Roles, Rules, and Responses

1. Joseph Biuso and Brian Newman with Gary Wilde, *Receiving Love* (Wheaton, Ill.: Victor Books, 1996), 44.

2. Therese A. Rando, *Grieving: How to Go On Living When Someone You Love Dies* (Lexington, Mass.: Lexington Books, 1988), 121-5, adapted.

Chapter 7: It's Different for Them: A Look at Age Differences

1. Therese A. Rando, *Grieving: How to Go on Living When Someone You Love Dies* (Lexington, Mass.: Lexington Books, 1988), 200-4, adapted.

Chapter 8: Think Their Thoughts

1. James A. Fogarty, *The Magical Thoughts of Grieving Children: Treating Children with Complicated Mourning and Advice for Parents* (Amityville, N.Y.: Baywood, 2000), 160, adapted.

2. Therese A. Rando, *Grieving: How to Go on Living When Someone You Love Dies* (Lexington, Mass.: Lexington Books, 1988), 218.

Chapter 9: Feel Their Feelings Too

1. Joseph Braga and Laurie Braga, *Children and Adults: Activities for Growing Together* (Englewood Cliffs, N.J.: Prentice-Hall, 1976), 262-4, adapted.

2. Louise Desport, "1946 Desperate Fables," *American Journal of Orthopsychiatry* (January 16): 100-3.

Chapter 10: Help Them Get Unstuck

1. Martha Wakenshaw, *Caring for Your Grieving Child* (Oakland, Calif.: New Harbinger, 2002), 127, adapted.

2. Carol Staudacher, *Beyond Grief: A Guide for Recovering from the Death of a Loved One* (Oakland, Calif.: New Harbinger, 1987), 151.

Chapter 11: Depression: When Feelings Get "Stuffed"

1. William Lee Carter, *KidThink* (Dallas: Word, Rapha, 1992), 142, adapted.

2. Carter, *KidThink*, 134-5.

Chapter 12: Divorce: A Never-Ending Grief

1. Archibald D. Hart, *Children and Divorce: What to Expect, How to Help* (Waco: Word, 1982), 66-74, adapted.

Chapter 13: Trauma: It Shouldn't Happen to a Child

1. Robin Karr-Morse and Meredith S. Wiley, *Ghosts from the Nursery: Tracing the Roots of Violence* (New York: Atlantic Monthly Press, 1997), 159, 163, adapted.

2. Kendall Johnson, *Trauma in the Lives of Children* (Alameda, Calif.: Hunter House, 1998), 46-7, adapted.

3. Johnson, *Trauma,* 63, adapted.

To learn more about WaterBrook Press and view our catalog of products, log on to our Web site:
www.waterbrookpress.com

WATERBROOK
PRESS